Tomorrowland:

Scenarios for law firms beyond the horizon

first edition

I

BRUCE MACEWEN

Adam Smith, Esq.®
New York
2017

ALSO BY BRUCE MACEWEN

GROWTH IS DEAD: NOW WHAT?
LAW FIRMS ON THE BRINK (2012)

A NEW TAXONOMY:
THE SEVEN LAW FIRM BUSINESS MODELS (2014)

Published by Adam Smith, Esq., LLC
305 West 98th Street
New York, New York 10025
USA

Library of Congress Cataloging-in-Publication Data is available
ISBN-13:978-154304947

Composed and published at New York, New York.

Printed in the United States of America

Cover design and graphics by faucethead

Audiobook narration by Matt Haynes

For Mac

What People Are Saying

Some early reactions to *Tomorrowland*:

"Must reading for every law firm managing partner, for every law firm partner, and for anyone interested in the future of Big Law. Extraordinarily well done and insightful; courageous and audacious. A tour de force."

—Brad Karp,
Chair of the Firm, Paul Weiss

"Covers some big territory very well and tests the edges of what is comfortable. Thoughtful and challenging; motivates the reader to pause and think, in spades."

—Mark Rigotti,
Chief Executive Officer, Herbert Smith Freehills

"No self-respecting law firm leader should be prepared to run the risk of leaving it unread."

—Charles Martin,
Senior Partner, Macfarlanes

"Masterful—a convergence of a lifetime of learning, and not just between the white lines of the legal industry."

—Peter Kalis,
Chairman and Global Managing Partner, K&L Gates

"A model is never defeated by facts, however damaging, but only by another model."

—Albert O. Hirschman,
Exit, Voice, and Loyalty
(Harvard University Press: 1970) at 68

Contents

Charles Martin, Senior Partner, Macfarlanes

The animal kingdom is not full of role models when it comes to adapting and looking to the future. Some think that the calm oblivion of the ostrich is attractive. The dodo is no longer around to offer much guidance, which in a way speaks for itself. The chameleon does pretty well but might be thought to lack a consistent strategic vision. And, of course, the frog famously will stay put in a beaker of water over a Bunsen burner until it is boiled alive. Perhaps the black swan or its close relative the flying pig are the most valuable guides to the future. As Bruce indeed suggests in the Introduction.

The ever-increasing and multi-dimensional complexity of the Rubik's cube that is the business world and all the risks that flow from it are comforting prospective sources of work for lawyers as they ponder a future in which almost everything will change. A future in which some unknown proportion of what they do today will be done by artificial intelligence, in which clients will continue increasingly to be calling the shots and will have independent access to all the legal knowledge that they need and in which a relentless increase in pricing pressure will be one of the few things that any informed observer would predict with confidence. Amongst the other likely constant features are pervasive ambiguity and uncertainty.

Yet, for all this confusion, law firm leaders need to understand the huge range of factors, reflect on their impact on their own particular firm and respond in a way that appropriately discharges the responsibilities which their partners have entrusted them with. What are the qualities needed to do this? The ideal leader will have original ideas, will be outstanding at listening to clients as well as being empathetic, flexible and responsive (but not unquestioningly so) to internal pressures. He/she will run a tight ship financially and will be adept at coping with the inherent contradictions and ambiguities that I have already touched on.

So when a book that explores all of this through thoughtful scenarios and which offers deep insights into the legal market borrowing from a wide range of perspectives and academic thinking emerges, no self-respecting law firm leader should be prepared to run the risk of leaving it unread. Too often books about the future of the legal industry offer overly simplistic views of where things will go. That is, in a way, even more surprising when one reflects on how rarely past predictions have proved accurate. Only global law firms will survive. The mid-tier firm has no future. Gender diversity will inexorably improve rather than getting stuck. The billable hour will be gone within a decade. And so on.

It is also fashionable for commentators to be fundamentally gloomy in their vision for the legal industry. Bruce's thesis is a highly challenging, but an inherently stimulating and exciting one. Not one that is complacent in any way but one that points to a small number of fundamental truths.

Lawyers and the competitive advantage that their distinctive governance and organisational structures give them have something that offers a robust and enduring formula for success. But the trick is in attracting true talent (which is ever more mobile and unconstrained by the status quo) and organising it with clarity of purpose and message. Then communicating that message through a clear and consistent brand. This is a formula which, whilst ephemeral and calling for constant evolution, is likely to meet enduring client needs.

Bruce suggests that incumbency is unlikely of itself to offer as much advantage in the future as it has done historically. He points to the power of insurgency and focusses on possibly the most fundamental change in the dynamics of the legal industry over the last decades – namely that it is not about lawyers and law firms but clients and the fitness of law firms to respond to their changing needs.

The reader should be prepared to be challenged because the problems that Bruce tackles are complex and intellectually interesting. Unusually Bruce borrows as much from science, history and literature as he does from the business school thinking that is so often directly and uneasily applied to the legal industry.

The reader should not expect to find a roadmap to success in this book. Neither should he/she expect to agree with everything that Bruce has written. However, every law firm leader who reads this book will come away with a new perspective on the future of the legal industry and the threats, opportunities and possibilities that will emerge. And all readers will come away with a to-do list that is longer and richer than before.

Charles Martin
London

Introduction

The future may be unknowable, but it's not unthinkable.

This book is intended to help you think about the future.

Thinking about the future is quite different from predicting the future—it's unknowable, remember—but that scarcely means we're helpless or without tools in this endeavor. This book is such a tool.

I write specifically about possible futures for sophisticated law firms—"Law Land"—but I believe the approach I take and the techniques I'll apply could be extrapolated without violent distortion to inquiries into possible futures for many other professions, especially those that operate primarily on the home turf of business-to-business commerce.

Scenarios are at the heart of this book. A scenario is not a prediction. A scenario is a mental model, a powerful one I believe, for delving into the question, "If this (current or nascent) trend or phenomenon continues or accelerates in operation, what would the world then look like?"

Scenarios also provide the book with its structure. As you'll see, I will propose a series of different scenarios, each of which—were it the only evolutionary force at work—would define strongly if not dictate outright where Law Land is going. Do not underestimate this. Indeed, I'll remind you of and underscore the power of any single scenario, operating unchecked and in isolation, to dominate events through the straightforward and direct matter of chapter titles: I give each scenario one chapter where it "wins."

Proceeding as if one and only one scenario will "win," of course, would be too easy. Come to think of it, in that case I might be able to get away with a single chapter devoted to the winner—why trouble ourselves with the also-ran's? Unfortunately that would bring us right back to you, Dear Reader, proceeding with this book in the expectation that I will be advancing predictions and your job is merely to follow along. Wrong, and wrong.

First, I will not be offering predictions because, aside from the obvious awkwardness should they prove to be mistaken as time unfolds, I find predictions self-referential; they inevitably seem to map the writer's own self-centered view of the world into the indefinite future in a brute-force, linear fashion. Understand that we all have such views and that this is not the core of the problem. The problem as I see it is that once one understands the writer's premises, you tend to learn little more by ploughing through the volume.

This brings us to the second expectation I labeled "wrong:" Do not expect to read this book in passive "receive mode"—not, at least, if you want to extract the most value from it. I understand that advising you on the attitude with which you should approach this book may seem presumptuous, and at the very least a bit of an imposition, but that's the way scenarios work.

Scenarios have another advantage in helping us think about how the future might unfold. We tend to find ourselves trapped by the temptation to default to a linear extrapolation of what's recently just occurred: It's tough to escape the assumptive box that "the best predictor of the weather tomorrow is the weather today."

This simplistic approach turns out to be improbably accurate when it comes to the weather, but it's wildly fallacious when it comes to human behavior and the ways of the world. Yes, the groundwork for any given scenario ought to be discernible in conditions as they are today—I find it a sturdy guide to try to stay in touch with reality whenever possible—but no scenario takes today's conditions at face value and more pointedly, none follows Alexander Pope's counsel that "whatever is, is right" (*An Essay on Man*, I.292 [1733—'34]).

That said, if you are now on the verge of despairing of finding even one prediction in this book, here you go: This will be my first and last, but one I stand behind with a high degree of confidence: The world is far too complex for any one-dimensional scenario to win.

Here are a few ways the world is too "complex:"

- We will experience many surprising exogenous economic and political shocks. That they'll be "exogenous" implies they'll be harder to see coming. Nassim Nicholas Taleb famously labeled these as "black swans," events that have a major impact, come as a complete surprise, and which people often attempt, fecklessly, to rationalize in hindsight. Black swans:

- o Are rare, high-impact events that normal expectations in finance, science, technology, and political theory cannot predict or account for;
- o Thanks to the essential nature of tiny probabilities, escape normal calculations of likelihood; and
- o Exploit our psychological biases, which blind us to an accurate understanding of uncertainty and the massive impact of rare events.

- Technology will develop in unforeseeable and, in a profound sense, unimaginable ways. Imagine showing a smartphone to Thomas Jefferson, or for that matter Dwight Eisenhower, and asking them to guess how its technology works and what it can do. This illustrates Arthur C. Clarke's postulate that "any sufficiently advanced technology is indistinguishable from magic." We may think we live in the post-Steve Jobs era, but viewed differently we're living in the pre-Benjamin Franklin era.

- Social mores, customs, and assumptions about such bedrock institutions as work, family, religion, sexuality, and education will, if the past few decades are any guide, soon make today's received wisdom seem primitive and unsuitable for polite society, even contemptible.

- The ongoing struggles between liberty and authority, spontaneous bottom-up and technocratic top-down organizing principles, and meritocratic vs. egalitarian societies, will continue to play out unabated. Contrary to "end of history" buffs, you can trace this debate forward from Plato through Locke, Hume, and Rousseau, to Kant and Nietzsche, and lately even to John Rawls and Richard Dawkins, with no sign of its impending resolution.

- And competitors, rivals, clients, and talented professionals within your industry or adjacent to it will react to all of the above in unforeseeable ways.

In reality, the word "complexity" fails to do justice to why the future will never play out quite as we might have liked to imagine. The shortcoming of invoking "complexity," in isolation, is that we tend to view it as a *spatial* characteristic of the world—technology in this corner, shocks and black swans erupting from that corner, special interests in their own Venn diagram bubbles, etc.—and we ignore the all-important dimension of *time:* If one condition changes, it is intellectually and analytically impermissible to assume no other conditions will change in response.

The military has a nice phrase for this: "The enemy gets a vote."

Or, completing our geometric analogy, the world is not only three-dimensional, it is dynamic.

A tributary of economic thinking that went sadly ignored for nearly a century, and is now enjoying an overdue and well-deserved renascence, is typically referred to as the concept of "radical uncertainty," and whether or not that term fires your memory neurons, that's what we've been talking about for the past few pages.

Frank Knight (1885—1972), a University of Chicago economics professor, published *Risk, Uncertainty, and Profit* in 1921 (Boston: Houghton Mifflin), which introduced the world to the distinction between "risk" and "uncertainty:"

> "Uncertainty must be taken in a sense radically distinct from the familiar notion of Risk, from which it has never been properly separated.... The essential fact is that 'risk' means in some cases a quantity susceptible of measurement, while at other times it is something distinctly not of this character; and there are far-reaching and crucial differences in the bearings of the phenomena depending on which of the two is really present and operating.... It will appear that a measurable uncertainty, or 'risk' proper, as we shall use the term, is so far different from an unmeasurable one that it is not in effect an uncertainty at all."

Indeed, "radical uncertainty" is by some referred to interchangeably as "Knightian uncertainty." Examples can be useful in drawing the risk/uncertainty distinction, and a few common ones are insuring your home against fire (a "risk," with a calculable policy premium associated with it, which actuaries will happily specify for you) vs. asking whether nuclear fusion will be a significant source of electricity generation by 2040. Where to begin?

Similarly, airlines and regulatory authorities can calculate the likelihood of a fatal crash per X million passenger-miles, but what the economics of the airline industry will look like in (say) 2040 and who the major carriers will be, pursuing what business models? Not a prayer.

Keynes himself not only fully appreciated Knight's insights, but extended their implications to conventional economic analysis in *The General Theory of Employment, Interest, and Money*:[1]

> Our knowledge of the factors which will govern the yield of an investment some years hence is usually very slight and often negligible. If we speak frankly, we have to admit that our basis of knowledge for estimate the yield ten years hence of a railway, a copper mine, a textile factory, the goodwill of a patent medicine, an Atlantic liner, a building in the City of London amounts to little and sometimes to nothing; or even five years hence.
>
> By 'uncertain' knowledge, let me explain, I do not mean merely to distinguish what is known for certain from what is merely probable. The game of roulette is not subject, in this sense, to uncertainty. [The] expectation of life is only slightly uncertain [and] even the weather is only moderately uncertain.
>
> The sense in which I am using the term is that in which the prospect of a European war is uncertain, or the price of copper and the rate of interest twenty years hence, or the obsolescence of a new invention. About these matters there is no scientific basis on which to form any calculable probability whatever. We simply do not know.

---

1 (London: Palgrave Macmillan) 1st ed. 1936, at 113-114..

Nevertheless, the necessity for action and for decision compels us as practical men to overlook this awkward fact and to behave exactly as we should if we had behind us a good Benthamite calculation of a series of prospective advantages and disadvantages, each multiplied by its appropriate probability, waiting to be summed.

Mervyn King, chair of the Bank of England from 2003 to 2013, adopts radical uncertainty as his core idea in his book on the great financial crisis, *The End of Alchemy: Money, Banking, and the Future of the Global Economy* (W. W. Norton, New York: 2016). He's also careful to distinguish radical uncertainty from behavioral economics, to which it bears a casual resemblance:

The danger in the assumption of behavioural economics that people are intrinsically irrational is that it leads to the view that governments should intervene to correct "biases" in individual decisions or to "nudge" them towards optimal outcomes.

But why do we feel able to classify behavior as irrational? Are policy-makers more rational than the voters whose behavior they wish to modify? I prefer to assume that neither group is stupid but that both are struggling to cope with a challenging environment. [...]

The problem with behavioural economics is that it does not confront the deep question of what it means to be rational when the assumptions of the traditional optimizing model fail to hold. Individuals are not compelled to be driven by impulses, but nor are they living in a world for which there is a single optimizing solution to each problem.

If we do not know how the world works, there is no unique right answer, only a problem of coping with the unknown.[2]

I would ask you, then, Dear Reader, to proceed with the book in your hands with the notion of radical uncertainty as something of an organizing principle. Risk lends itself to quantification and indeed to

---

2   *Alchemy* at p. 133-134.

mind-bending equations and economic models, but radical uncertainty is mathematically intractable.

Perhaps that's why economists tried to ignore it for nearly a century; they didn't know quite what to do with it.

This is not the time or place to speculate about the future course of academic and popular economic thinking, but permit me to note that taking radical uncertainty seriously demands a profound rethink of conventional economic analysis. To begin with, rather than postulate a rational *homo economicus* as the kicking-off point for analysis, convenient because utility-maximizing functions and indifference frontiers lend themselves to standard techniques in algebra and geometry, the intellectual task would be of a different order altogether.

Under radical uncertainty, people, firms, and nations leave the realm of dealing with quantifiable risks and move directly into "coping."

Which brings us back to scenarios and not predictions. Predictions are grounded in (usually fallacious) calculations of probabilities; scenarios ask us to imagine how we as individuals and leaders of firms would cope "if....."

So with this introduction and counsel, shall we begin?

Slip your critical faculties into gear, and I'll preview the scenarios to follow. I have not arranged their sequence and presentation in any particular structured or principled order or along any spectrum from "most ___" to "least ___" or vice versa, so don't be disconcerted if you find no such flow. My goal, to the extent the sequence is purposeful at all, is primarily to keep the perspectives appearing fresh. Logic compels only the first and the last to appear where they are.

Nothing to see here, folks; move along
Lawyer psychology, enabled by the partnership model, wins
Talent and free agency win
Differentiation and "speciation" win
New entrants win
Networks win
Brands win
Machines win
The dynamics of market evolution.

"Doubt is not a pleasant condition,
but certainty is an absurd one."

—Voltaire, Letter to Frederick William, Prince of Prussia,
28 November 1770, Tallentyre, S.G. (ed.), Voltaire in His Letters
(New York: G. P. Putnam's Sons, 1919) at 28.

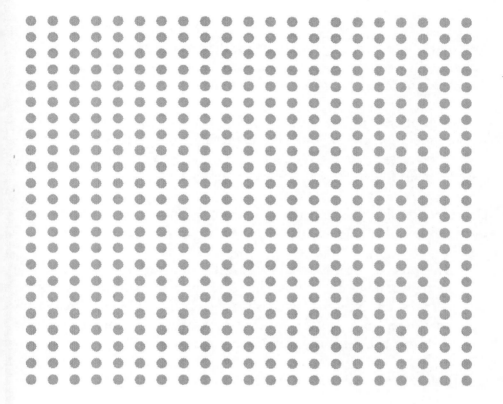

Nothing To See Here, Folks; Move Along

I of course steal the cliché police use to discourage crowds from congregating at a crime scene, and use it to symbolize the view that nothing new is really happening in Law Land and nothing needs to change--so what's all the fuss about? The Cravath Model has served us well for over 100 years. Can't you see that many firms remain a license to print money? Law firms are scarcely the newspaper industry or the photographic film industry; there's nothing to be alarmed about. Relax, young man; quiet down.

This deserves to be our first scenario for the most basic of reasons: At the outset of this venture together it's salutary to be reminded that at least in this corner of the world the future need not look drastically different.

The assumption that Law Land "just *has to* change," usually expressed with exasperation and an implicit unflattering view of on the intelligence of the one the exclamation is directed towards, has, at least based on developments to date, scant evidence to support it.

Consider how little has changed in terms of the fundamental structure of the law firm industry (presented in no particular order of importance):

A. The ranks of the marquee players in the industry have experienced incremental but not seismic change in their ranks over the past few decades: The New York white shoe elite, London's Magic Circle, a few newcomers more notable for their rarity than their ubiquity (Latham, Kirkland, a few litigation-centric powerhouses).

B. Our revenue and pricing model is still fundamentally the same: The billable hour.

C. The core career path within firms is unchanged: Associate to partner. No other status or title matters.

   Yes, contract/staff/temp positions have multiplied and are continuing to do so, the disagreeable coinage "non-partner track" is now part of the *lingua franca*, and the onshore-nearshore-offshore phenomenon seems to be spreading without letup, but all those developments are viewed as peripheral and not what the *real* essence of the firm is all about, certainly not to those in the know.

D. Without material exception, lawyers—not business executives—still run law firms and in all but the most exceptionally enlightened firms, business professionals in finance, operations, IT, marketing, and all the other functions sophisticated organizations require are unthinkingly and unconsciously labeled "non-lawyers," not given a seat or more importantly a voice at the Big Table, and marginalized when real decisions need to be made.[3]

E. The partnership structure remains the essentially universal organizing model—not an equity-based corporate structure, which prevails in the other 98% of the economy.

In a way, the first four of these—embedded name brands at the top, our revenue/pricing model, career path, and lawyers in charge—are the subject of the remainder of the book. More precisely, the book implicitly lines these up as the ground on which each of the scenarios plays out and invites you to assess how or whether each survives. So I shall say little more about each of them explicitly. For now, they represent the air we breathe in Law Land—78% nitrogen, 21% oxygen, 1% everything else. Duly noted.

The partnership structure, on the other hand, is a potent beast, and like any powerful force it can wreak destruction and even turn sinister. I'll devote a fair amount of space to it in the next Chapter, where the implications of this form fit hand in glove with lawyer psychology—and not, I'll suggest, in a promising fashion.

• • •

Perhaps we should begin our exploration of this scenario by turning the premise on its head: How could it be that a sophisticated, quintessentially

---

3   You have to admit this is bizarre.

Across the entire span of the rest of the economy, you will find nowhere else the undiluted homogeneity that's universal in the ranks of law firm management. Fortune 1000 and FTSE 100 firms are run by professionals from finance, marketing, engineering, operations, sales, and even (still) the occasional mailroom alum. But suggest such diversity to a law firm?

Compounding the sheer weirdness of this ubiquitous management structure is that many managing partners take pride in continuing to practice law—as if Jeff Immelt at GE had to prove his bona fides by daily stints in the thick of jet engine design and engineering.

But never mind, because lawyers of course know best. Better than all of them.

knowledge-intensive, global industry, serving demanding clients with the brainpower of highly sophisticated and analytic Type A professionals, could not materially change in the 21st Century? And more importantly, would not need to?

For the best evidence, simply look at the track record of Law Land over the past, say, 50 years. The Cravath System, still the irreducible hard core of conventional Big Law's business model, has shown itself to be an extremely robust profit-spinning machine. From (say) 1980 up until the Great Financial Meltdown of 2008, Big Law didn't merely keep pace with the global rising tide, it turned in decade after decade of supra-normal growth in revenue, headcount, and profitability: An impressive run that almost any CEO in the other 98% of the economy would envy.

Even in the sluggish post-meltdown decade of the 2010's, BigLaw's growth rates of revenue and of profits remain comfortably above the US corporate average.[4] So long as Law Land continues to deliver these results, the case for urgent and drastic change will strike most of those in a position to actually make it happen—the leaders of law firms—as somewhere between alarmist and delusional.

A host of structural factors point towards the same outcome of fundamental stasis.

Let's take the five I opened with in order:
   A. Stable ranks of the elite firms;
   B. The billable hour;
   C. Career paths;
   D. Lawyers in charge; and
   E. The partnership as organizational form.

A. Stable ranks of the elite

Stability at the top of the food chain of an industry indicates that clients are by and large satisfied with their providers and conversely that the providers are happy to continue tending to their knitting and making healthy profit margins in the process, as they always have.

---

4   The US Bureau of Economic Analysis has a wealth of data on "National Economic Accounts" including these series. See generally: http://www.bea.gov/national/index.htm

Consider the counterfactual: We would only see substantial or rapid turnover among the ranks of the elite firms if clients were dissatisfied enough to vote with their feet in large numbers and/or if the firms were finding their tried and true business model had seriously broken down in performing its two critical functions: (a) attracting sophisticated clients with the wherewithal, and the willingness, to pay elite rates and fees; and (b) being able to continue to recruit, develop, filter, and shed or retain the essential top-tier talent which constitutes the bedrock supply for these firms. Since we see no change, the simplest and most direct explanation is that all parties to this bargain at the top feel their needs are being well-served and are content. Otherwise we'd see turmoil in the rankings, and we don't.

Another powerful factor is in play here: To be treated as an elite firm, both by marquee clients (demand) and potential talent in the form of lawyers with elite educations and sophisticated expertise (supply), you need to already have a reputation as an elite firm. I'm not being cute— to the contrary.

But ours is an industry with essentially no objective, quantitative measures of quality. Determining where a law firm ranks on the quality spectrum therefore becomes a conversation held in an echo chamber. The only points of reference one can attempt to seize onto are, circularly, characteristics of "Quality" itself:

- Pre-existing reputation (see the problem already?);

- Lawyers' pedigree—reputation of undergraduate college/university and law school;

- Word of mouth; and

- Experience with previous high-caliber, high-stakes matters.

All of these are self-referential and circular. Pre-existing reputation speaks for itself, but lawyers' pedigree is conceptually the same: Lawyers with the highest possible conventional credentials (US Supreme Court clerks, Law Review at a Top 10 or Top 5 law school) *know* which firms their peers and predecessors have gone to or are interviewing with, and only firms that have some non-trivial critical mass of people with this caliber of credentials can plausibly seek to recruit more like them.

Word of mouth? Check.

Experience with previous, comparable high-stakes matters? Circular to be sure, but it's even worse than that: You won't be in the consideration set for these matters unless you've already been in the consideration set for these matters.

Bottom line: Stability should be no surprise.

B. The billable hour

Here we have a very long, borderline notorious, history of predictions of the imminent demise of the billable hour failing to pan out, only to be resuscitated, failing to pan out, and [repeat]. Defensively, I feel constrained to report to you that I have never been one of the billable hour's wannabe executioners, but I do believe its market share has peaked (that is to say, the share of law firm revenue derived from this revenue model has peaked).

Setting this checkered forecasting history aside, what can we say about the billable hour as a revenue model?

For starters, it's a cost-plus model, meaning profit is built in, assuming only that you can collect a substantial percentage of the stated hourly rate. The primary consequence of cost-plus models in the marketplace is that they shift all risk—of unanticipated developments, scope creep, necessary on-the-job learning, and life's surprises in general—from the provider to the client. From a law firm's perspective, what could be better?

The other salient economic reality of the billable hour is that it's grounded on "cost of production (inputs)," not "value to client (outputs)." In the abstract, this is upside-down; value to client ought of right to be the primary if not the only determinant of price. This brings to mind Ben Bernanke's famous remark in October 2014:

Just before leaving the Fed this year, Mr Bernanke was asked if he was confident in advance that QE – the policy of buying bonds to drive down long-term interest rates when short-term rates are already at zero – would do the job. Mr Bernanke replied: "The problem with QE is it works in practice, but it doesn't work in theory."[5]

So with the billable hour: In purist economic theory it makes no sense, but it works magnificently in practice.

So we have a fundamental revenue model that shifts all execution risk from the firm-provider to the client-buyer while ensuring the firm a profit at the cost of radical unpredictability for the client, that is premised on what should be an irrelevancy (cost of production), but which seemingly has 99 lives.

Clearly it's proven to be a robust revenue model for Law Land, I think for two reasons.

First, it's easy to propose "value to client" or "output" as the lodestar, but how on earth does one measure that? When the value of output is unquantifiable, the cost of inputs comes immediately to mind. Not highly defensible, but at least understandable.

Second and with even more powerful results: Clients seem to be perfectly comfortable with it. Time and again I've heard lawyers recount tales of submitting complex and sophisticated "alternative fee arrangement" proposals to clients only to have the client back out at the end, with words to the effect, "just give us a discount off the rack rate instead." If clients aren't willing to change, we never should and never will force them to do otherwise. Long live the billable hour!

C. Career paths

Unique among professional service firms, Law Land still envisions itself as subscribing internally to a two-caste up-or-out career track for its professionals: Younger lawyers enter as associates until after X number of years a symbolic gong is rung and the chosen few are elevated to partner, while the rest must leave, sooner or later.

---

5   Widely reported at the time, but see, for example, "US quantitative measures worked in defiance of theory," *Financial Times* (October 13, 2014) at https://www.ft.com/content/3b164d2e-4f03-11e4-9c88-00144feab7de

I rehearse this commonplace only because, stated baldly, it comes across as an odd talent development and retention system indeed—but it is *our* system and as much as novelties like income or non-equity partners, staff lawyers, partner-track and non-partner-track associates, have encroached from the edges and diluted its purity, it remains our aspirational ideal.[6]

I mentioned this was an "odd" format for a career path meant to carry one for a lifetime, and I intended that word in two complementary sense: First, it's statistically an anomaly. If you look across the broad swath of other industries in the economy—corporate land to be sure, with its innumerable gradations of assistant that and senior this, but also other professional services sectors—nobody else does it the way we do it. That we know better than everyone else, they're wrong and we're right, has to be entered in the consideration set of all possible explanations, but it wouldn't be where the betting money would go.

But second and more fundamentally, it's "odd" in the plain old sense that it's weird. Law firms traditionally invested richly in summer clerks and junior associates, and even as the scale of those programs have been sanely pared back, the strangest feature remains intact: Just as the youngish lawyer is prepared to transition from worker bee to autonomous professional with sound judgment, we ask almost all of them either to leave

---

6   Prof. Bill Henderson of Indiana/Maurer School of Law, the appropriately celebrated *sui generis* analyst of Law Land, and (disclosure) a friend, published *The Diamond Law Firm: A New Model or the Pyramid Unraveling?* in 2013. Using 35 years of NLJ 250 data, he demonstrated that the simple ratio of associates to partners peaked nearly a quarter century earlier, and that since 2008 partners (both equity and non-equity combined) have actually outnumbered associates in total, with the lines continuing to diverge since then, partner headcount upward and associate headcount downward.

As Bill stated drily, "this may surprise many industry insiders" and argued that much of the invisibility of this development could be attributed not just to the power of the simple "pyramid" mental model, but to its unintended and almost accidental roots: " its emergence is likely less a product of careful strategy deliberations than a series of short-term, ad hoc responses designed to deal with harsh and unfamiliar market conditions."

See http://www.lawyermetrics.org/2013/12/03/the-diamond-law-firm-a-new-model-or-the-pyramid-unraveling/

or to accept second-class citizenship as a non-equity. We cultivate talent at great lengths only to discard or demoralize it at the moment of ripeness.[7]

Let's pick up the thread here, shall we? Remember the rules: This is the Scenario where nothing changes, and nothing actually needs to change: Steady as she goes. So why am I discussing—using incontrovertible empirical data—how the traditional two-tier partner:associate model is breaking down?

Because it's not really breaking down at all.

First and foremost, it is still, as Bill Henderson would warmly agree, the mental model we all have in mind to describe the internal career path at firms for lawyers. Second, while we've been picking at its fraying edges and tweaking here and there, we haven't remotely ripped it out root and branch. Doing that would mean adopting, say, something like the McKinsey career model, where the array of choices starts with a selection among half a dozen consulting discipline (strategy, research, analytics, implementation, turnaround, digital) and overlays that with one of 22 industry specializations (advanced electronics, aerospace & defense, automotive & assembly, etc., through travel, transport & logistics).[8]

Through these and other permutations, McKinsey claims there are "500+ roles available." *That* would be root and branch change. And might we stipulate that McKinsey is probably not naïve when it comes to organizing a sophisticated professional service firm?

Permit me to conclude this section with an observation about psychology. Law firm career paths won't change until partners want them to. They don't. They're the Brahmin caste. And many feel they lived through their own Parris Island boot camp experience as a lowly associate and proudly came out on top; why make it easier, or even different, for the younger generation?

---

7   It's safe to say "almost all" have to leave or accept the second-best of non-equity, because the percentage of all lawyers at NLJ 250 firms who were full equity partners peaked in the early 1990's and has been in slow and steady decline ever since. Recent years have seen the ranks of the equity grow in the range of +1.0% to -0.5%. No wonder younger lawyers talk morbidly but inarguably of having to wait for someone to retire, or die.

8   See *McKinsey & Company,* http://www.mckinsey.com/careers/explore-mckinsey

D. Lawyers in charge

Lawyers run law firms, and not just at the Managing Partner or Chair level, where one can at least understand, if not endorse, the value of having a senior colleague who's come up through the same ranks you have, at the head of the firm. I'm not talking about that: Lawyers tend to run law firms from top to bottom and from left to right, across all functional disciplines. It matters not whether they have any formal, or even on-the-job, training in (say) finance, marketing, or HR; the business professionals who might head those functions on paper are answerable in the real world to the partners.

And in most law firms, answerable to pretty much any and all partners at any time. Most partners assume their entitlement to second-guess most business professionals, and most business professionals realize they need to be prepared to account for their actions whenever a partner speaks up. This is so ubiquitous in law firms that most people hardly notice it any more, or if they do, assume that of course that's so and all's right with the world. All is not right; this is a wretched way to run a business.

Expert poker players are always looking for other players at the table to reveal a "tell"—a funny tic, motion, or fleeting facial expression that the expert interprets, through experience, as giving insight into the strength or weakness of the other player's hand. A "tell" stands for a something that is tiny and unintended but deeply revealing.

I submit that that a tell for how universal the abominable subordination of business professionals is, is the word "non-lawyer." It indelibly categorizes and demeans, yet countless people employ it thoughtlessly and by reflex. The business professional's training, experience, and pedigree are irrelevant; they're not lawyers.

True story: An AmLaw 50 firm decided a few years ago, smartly, to launch an ambitious client relationship program, and hired a new-to-Law Land individual whose immediate former job was managing a global account for a communications agency's largest and most profitable single client, representing $25-million/year in revenue to the agency and served by a client team of 100 people in 30 countries. Amply qualified, you would think.

Many of the partners begged to differ, asking the client relationship director point-blank what they could possibly offer the partner, since the director wasn't a lawyer.

You can guess how many, or how few, times our professional friend had to hear challenges like this before there came a parting of the ways. (This story also give us a window into the truly impressive depths of lawyerly insecurity, but I invite you to engage in that discussion at home.)

It is zero distance from this type of story—which could be repeated at almost any AmLaw 200 firm you pick by throwing darts at the rankings—to understanding the low expectations partners have for business professionals and business professionals' own frustration at this demeaning treatment. And when the businessperson gets fed up and leaves, partners shrug and reconfirm their low expectations, doubly damning the businessperson's replacement, and so on.

As with our career paths discussion, call this the height of irrationality but partners are overwhelmingly comfortable with it—if they're even conscious of their behavior. Fully expect nothing to change on this score.

E. The partnership as organizational form

This brings us to the partnership as organizational form.

And that, Dear Reader, I actually address in the next chapter, because it's such a large topic in itself.

But a quick recap of Scenario 1 before we move on: Law firms will not fundamentally change because (a) they won't have to—their business model, which has proven itself so robust for a century, will proceed unruffled by clients' changing expectations, talent wars, new entrants, technology, or pretty much anything else; and (b) they would strongly and resolutely prefer not to.

We are deeply bound, intellectually, emotionally, and even as an expression of our identities, to the hierarchy of firms as we know it, to the Manichean partner/associate career path, to lawyers running law firms from north to south and east to west, and to the partnership form. We trust and believe that we will remain impervious in the face of future exogenous market forces, and we take immense pride in the structures we have created. Indeed, many of us would find it impossible to conceive what our lives would look like in a world without these pillars. Scenario 1 tells us we won't have to.

"A sound banker is not one who foresees danger and avoids it, but one who, when he is ruined, is ruined in a conventional and orthodox way with his fellows, so that no one can really blame him."

—John Maynard Keynes
(in his 1931 essay, The Consequences to the Banks of the Collapse of Money Values).

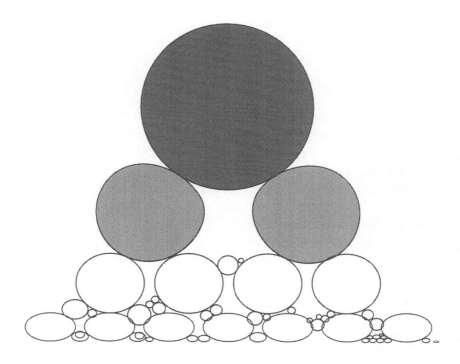

Lawyer Psychology and the Partnership Structure Win

In the first scenario and in this, law firms don't fundamentally change.

Certainly, they evolve and adopt new technology as it comes along, on the strict condition that their clients are also adopting it, like email, or at least on condition that their clients are approving or requiring it, like technology-assisted document review. Law firms also have and will continue to adopt new management practices once they've been refined, proven, and become ubiquitous elsewhere in the economy and among clients—more flexible working hours, at least rudimentary project management, more open and/or egalitarian office plans. But they'll be late adopters, grudging converts in their hearts. In the first scenario and this, all these developments are the same: Law firms do not *fundamentally* change.

The enormous difference is this: In Scenario 1, they don't have to change; business more or less as usual continues to work just fine. In this scenario, outside forces impose urgent requirements that they change, but they simply cannot bring themselves to do so. This scenario, in short, is populated by firms that would rather fail than change.

Lawyer Psychology

It's a commonplace, and the font of a thousand jokes, that many people don't trust lawyers. What may be less widely appreciated is that lawyers themselves often don't trust their own partners in their own firms.

Yes, I have personally encountered this staggering phenomenon, all too often. The most exquisitely distilled expression of how the inside of a law firm can be a trust-free zone was delivered by a partner who may—it's hard to tell—have thought he was being either clever or elusive, when I asked point-blank whether he trusted his partners: "The question isn't whether I trust any of them or not in fact; it's that *I don't want to have to trust* them."

You might think that in discussions about a firm's strategic direction, trust is secondary, a peripheral "nice to have," so long as competence and capability are a given.

Not so, at least not when it comes to communicating about critical topics, and we have a study out of Princeton University to prove it.[9] The authors polled adults about their views of common American jobs on the dimensions of "warmth" (trustworthiness) and "capability" (competence) and here are the results in a graphic nutshell:

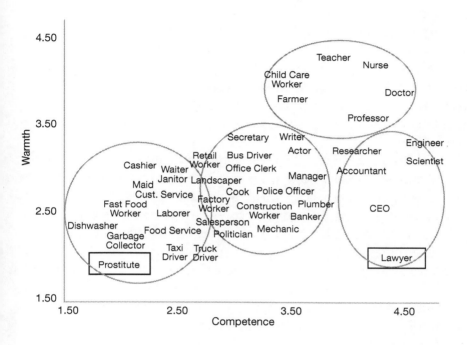

Readers may wish this were a joke, but it's not; lawyers rank on a par with prostitutes when it comes to trust. The authors label the cluster including lawyers, CEO's, accountants, etc., as "ambivalently perceived high-competence but low-warmth," and echo our thought that "being seen as competent but cold might not seem problematic, *until* one recalls that credibility requires not just status and expertise but also trustworthiness (warmth)." Why? Because "audiences view trustworthiness as the motivation to be truthful."

How can it be that in surprising numbers lawyers don't even trust each other?

---

9   Susan Fiske and Cydney Dupree, *Gaining trust as well as respect in communicating to motivated audiences about science topics,* Proceedings of the National Academy of Sciences of the United States of America (April 2014, available at http://www.pnas.org/content/111/Supplement_4/13593.abstract).

It's actually predictable: They were trained that way.

Dr. Larry Richard (a friend) is by all accounts the leading expert at the moment on, as he calls his online site, "what makes lawyers tick:" In other words, the singularly distinctive psychology of lawyers. Dr. Richard was a trial lawyer for ten years and then earned a Ph.D. in Psychology at Temple University; for the past 30 years he's worked with law firms on a range of "people issues."

Here's what he has to say (emphasis supplied) about lawyers and the personality trait labeled "skepticism," which is the opposite of a trusting nature. (People high in skepticism are low in trust and vice versa.)

> I've been gathering data on lawyers' personalities since the early 1980's. Personality traits are typically measured on a percentile scale ranging from zero % to 100%. When large samples of the general public are tested, individuals' scores on a given trait typically form a classic bell curve, with the mean average for any given trait hovering around the 50th percentile. But lawyers are different. As I have written about elsewhere, there are a number of traits on which lawyers tend to score much higher or much lower than the general public—in short, we're outliers. **The most extreme of all these outlier traits—the one on which lawyers consistently score higher (i.e., above the mean) than all the others—is Skepticism.**
>
> People with a very high Skepticism score tend to look at the world through a "glass half empty" lens—they focus on problems rather than on what's working well; they tend toward the suspicious; they assume the worst, and rarely give others the "benefit of the doubt". They wonder what another person's "real" motive might be for any action that person takes. They question any assertion made by another person. And they tend to be slower to trust others.
>
> [Skepticism is so high among lawyers,] first, because the personality trait of Skepticism provides an important advantage to any lawyer by making critical thinking more natural and easier. People with high levels of Skepticism are more likely to be attracted to the law in the first place. It feels more like a natural fit than many

other jobs might. ... So the legal profession starts out with an overrepresentation of skeptics ...

Second, for the same reason as above—i.e., the degree of "fit" between the person and the job—those lawyers with low Skepticism scores tend to drop out of law school and out of law practice (usually in their early years) at a higher rate than do those with high Skepticism scores. This "concentrates the herd" and results in a more overall skeptical cohort of lawyers who remain in practice.

Finally, Skepticism increases over time because lawyers work in a Skeptical environment. ... The longer a lawyer works in a workplace in which the majority of his/her colleagues think and talk in Skeptical ways, the more Skeptical s/he will become over time.

These three forces are all moving in the same direction. Over time, this becomes just the normal background "noise" and is taken for granted. Plus, **it's rare to find any counterbalancing force in most law firms that rewards "accepting" thinking or trusting behavior** (the opposites of Skepticism).[10]

Make no mistake, if you happen to be a client seeking a zealous advocate, Mr. Outlier-Skeptic is your go-to guy. You *want* someone who's suspicious, distrusting, questions any and all assertions, and harbors dark speculations about "real" motives.

And so the profession consistently turns out just such practitioners, by passing them, as it were, through a series of reverse osmosis filters until the distillate personality that emerges as partner in a major law firm has been quite rigorously purified. Thus: The more skeptical types (a) tend to be attracted to law school over other graduate pursuits; (b) do well there; (c) are hired into the more intense, high-performing law firms; (d) where they choose to stay; (e) and succeed; (f) becoming partners and even (g) leaders within the firm.

---

10   Dr. Larry Richard, *The Lawyer Personality: Why Lawyers Are Skeptical*, (15 November 2015), at http://www.abalcc.org/2015/11/16/the-lawyer-personality-why-lawyers-are-skeptical/

Some people have speculated that Millennials may score lower on skepticism and on "autonomy" (another trait where lawyers over-index conspicuously), implying that while this may be the state of the world today it won't be the state of the world forever. So I asked Dr. Richard about this and here's what he had to say:

> I do get asked this question a lot. So far, I literally see no changes. But the sample size is too small at this point to give me confidence in the data.
>
> However, this is actually exactly what I'd expect to see. Personality is more genetic, and there's no reason to expect different personalities to be entering the legal profession at this point unless law schools begin changing their admissions standards, which they haven't. (Even though the kinds of skills needed by today's lawyers are dramatically different from those of 20 years ago.)
>
> By contrast, the attitudes of Millennials are largely socially learned. Just because a generation learned to focus on shorter time frames, or were continuously told they were "wonderful", or have been trained to have shorter attention spans and to be more multi-tasking, does not by itself necessarily cause any change in their underlying personality traits. It may affect their values, their attitudes, and their behaviors, but personality is the most stable of all these constructs, so I don't expect it to change.
>
> The "autonomy" issue is certainly an interesting one. If a person has high autonomy as a personality trait, but is trained to have a dependent attitude, that might lead to some serious internal conflict. I'll certainly keep the idea in mind.[11]

There you have it: Conceivably when Millennials reach critical mass in the profession, or the ranks of its leaders, we may see a mid-course correction in personality. But overall, not so likely.

Dr. Richard's research has unveiled a few other personality traits of lawyers which make them strong statistical outliers vis-à-vis the rest of the adult population ("strong" as in one or two standard deviations off the mean).

---

11   Email from Dr. Larry Richard, to author (May 2016) (on file with author).

Two that are particularly germane to today's discussion are that lawyers rank low on "resilience" and high on "urgency."

Resilience measures the ability to bounce back gracefully from failure or setbacks. Lawyers generally don't. They're prone to falling into nursing a wound, sulking, or becoming pessimistic or cynical. Now, as a red-blooded American—a country where the cardinal sin is not to be defeated but to fail to jump right back up again—I might take the attitude that that's their problem and what's wrong with them, anyway? Alas, one may not be able to get away with such a glib reaction because, as I see it, low resilience explains, and causes, much of lawyers' notorious risk-aversion. (Come to think of it, another rather un-American trait.)

How does this dynamic work?

I think it's straightforward. If you take failure hard, you will be more loathe than average to experiment with new approaches because you will (correctly) anticipate that if it doesn't work out you'll be dashed. Rather than the typical and healthy try—fail—learn-and-move-on, your experience will be try—fail—be-miserable.

So the prudent approach is not to try in the first place: To be, in other words, risk-averse.

Dr. Richard points out a subtlety: Resilience embodies two components, what you might think of as a "hardiness" or "thick-skinned" component, and a "bounce-back" dimension. We've mostly been discussing the bounce-back part, which is also what most of the popular literature about "grit" and its brethren emphasizes.

But the Caliper instrument is a bit more sensitive to the thick-skinned component. Speaking of lawyers in their professional role, what is their initial reaction to encountering adversity? Criticism of their work, being rejected for a matter or an assignment, being intentionally excluded from a key meeting, and so forth? They're liable to feel hurt and wounded and, worse, not do a very effective job of keeping their feelings to themselves.

They won't react or come across as a best-foot-forward, team player. This graceless and frankly immature reaction can do one in among colleagues more decisively than the somewhat more amorphous and less visible (lack of) bounce-back.

Urgency is also highly adaptive for those serving in or being groomed for client advocacy, but it can produce insufferable interpersonal behavior. Lawyers can be driven by a pressing desire to achieve results for a client (good), but in pursuing their solution insistently, can also treat others peremptorily and with condescension: "I've figured out the answer; what's taking you so long?" (dysfunctional).

Now let's add skepticism back in and see what precipitates. Instinctive, perhaps even unconscious, resistance to new proposals, because after all:

- I can find problems with *anything* (skepticism),

- And am eager to tell you about them right now, even if I have to shoulder others' opinions aside (urgency),

- All underscored by my knowing that if the new thing doesn't work out, I'll rue the day it came up (lack of resilience).

Not exactly a recipe for experimentation, innovation, or agility.

The Opposite of the Scientific Method

The scientific method has been the modus operandi of the natural sciences since at least the 17th Century, and is so familiar that we rarely think about what it actually consists in, its cumulative power over time, or other ways of evaluating alternatives and discovering how the world really works. Essentially, it starts with observations about the world, proposes one or more hypotheses about why things are as they are, and devises experiments to test whether what a given hypothesis predicts is in reality how the world behaves. An hypothesis is only as strong as the weight of the experiments vindicating what it foretells.

Lawyers' tradecraft and mindset turns the scientific method on its head, or perhaps more precisely, runs it in reverse. Lawyers do not begin as agnostics and end with the most likely description of reality, they begin with the conclusion they are advocating for and design or assert facts and principles to support their predetermined position.

Having to assert far-fetched or implausible notions of cause and effect is no deterrent. Indeed, pointing out what might *conceivably* happen, no matter how improbable or irrational, is a point of pride and the mark of a creative lawyerly thinker: They have spotted an issue and demonstrated their cleverness.

It gets worse. The scientific method posits that some of the most valuable questions one can ask of the world are those which one cannot, at the moment, answer. ("Why does milkmaids' exposure to cowpox seem to protect them against smallpox?" "Why does this penicillium mold kill adjacent bacteria?" "Dark matter constitutes nearly 85% of the total mass of the universe; what on earth is it actually?")

Lawyers, by contrast, do almost anything they can to avoid asking questions they do not know the answer to. This is a recipe for standing firm and stalwart wherever one is most comfortable, and constitutes the antithesis of curiosity.

Clients in the market for a fierce advocate might rationally prefer someone who views the world in the way most radically favorable to their interest, and plans to stick with that view in the teeth of contrary probabilities, but when it comes to conducting the law firm's own business, you can see how this stands in the way of creative or even incremental improvements.

More importantly in terms of this Scenario: The inbred psychology of lawyers—their essential nature by the time they're leaders and partners in firms—renders them virtually incapable of making serious changes, no matter how imperative they might be. In times of marketplace turbulence, lawyers are truly their own worst enemies.

A small but ubiquitous example: When presented with almost any proposed change in the way they do things, no matter how trivial, the first question the change-proponent is sure to receive is, "Who else is doing this?" Not "how might this advance my practice?" or "why do you think clients would prefer that?" or—heaven forbid what you'd expect to hear from an innovative business professional—"I hope no one else is doing this!" Stated simplistically, law firms prefer not to change until law firms have changed.

A final note on this point. The law firm market, both in the United States and the rest of the world, is highly fragmented, almost atomized compared to other global industries. Even the largest law firms have at most a 1% market share. Why does this matter? Because if systemic industry-wide change is to come, it accelerates matters greatly if one or two large-scale, conspicuous market leaders adopts a new posture. This dynamic has played out, for example, with airlines banning smoking, car companies making features like airbags and electronic stability control standard, and food suppliers labeling GMO ingredients—in each case, industry adoption was widespread before regulations required it, because recognized market leaders led the way. That's simply not plausible in Law Land; no firm commands enough visibility, on its own, to provide a compelling example to everyone else.

By now you have to be wondering what all this has to do with partnership as an organizing structure.

I believe the partnership form *as lived and experienced today* in the vast majority of law firms is also a powerful force reinforcing the status quo—no matter how strong the rational evidence suggesting a change of course might be. Partnership exerts its potent gravitational pull towards the most conservative approach through the mechanism of instilling a conviction in every partner that he/she is an owner, therefore has a voice, and therefore should be able to veto any proposal posing an upset to their preferred and established way of doing things.

Blend lawyer psychology and the partnership structure together, immerse in an environment requiring organizations to change, and you have the recipe for producing firms that will *behave as if* they prefer failure over reform. And denying that's their intent all the way to the end serves little purpose.

The Partnership Structure

Firms are still structured, organizationally, as partnerships, regardless of whether it continues to make sense in the 21st Century. Actually, hardly anyone even poses the question, although I have; I found the answer to be, essentially, "no, the partnership model is no longer is fit for purpose."

To be sure, the partnership form could not be more familiar, and you can rely on intoning the word itself to summon warm and fuzzy notions of inclusiveness, participatory democracy, having a voice and being heard, and of course ownership.

What follows goes into why I believe, as a profession and as an industry, that we need to move beyond that.

But first, an obligatory prefatory caveat:

> Should we expect partnership as organizational form to change any time soon? Not likely.

Nevertheless, in the spirit of George Bernard Shaw's aphorism about progress depending on adapting conditions to one's beliefs and not adapting oneself to surrounding conditions, let us proceed.[12]

The following discussion touches upon scale, the extreme degree of difficulty of sustaining a true partnership, partnerships in name only, ethics and career planning, and fragility.

Scale

As firms grow from small and simple to regional, national, and global— and from monoline practices to complex poly-functional organizations with expertise in dozens of specialties—maintaining a partnership structure requires the firm to embrace a fundamental flaw in the model: Partnerships don't scale.

In this sense, partnerships resemble families. Our idealized notion of a family is of an embracing zone of trust, generosity, acceptance, and shared fate. Whether or not this squares with reality as we've experienced it, it's the aspiration. Families and partnerships alike can be dysfunctional or they can provide powerful platforms for enabling and achieving one's goals. I'm not talking about how well a family or a partnership functions in fact: I'm talking about theoretical limits to scale of such organizing

---

12   "The reasonable man adapts himself to the conditions that surround him... The unreasonable man adapts surrounding conditions to himself... All progress depends on the unreasonable man."

structures. One can have five close family members, or maybe 10 or 15, but not 100, 500, or 1,000.

We've known this for a long time, of course, and the famous "Dunbar number" quantifies the number of meaningful relationships most people can have: The number is 150.

Dunbar's number is now firmly grounded in empirical research from disciplines ranging across anthropology, primate studies, military affairs, corporate management, and industrial and organizational psychology.

The eponymous Oxford evolutionary psychologist Robin Dunbar more or less stumbled across his famous number in the 1990's when he studied the Christmas-card-sending habits of the English (in a pre-social-media world). He meant to address the question not how many people someone knew, but how many they cared about—and the effort to send a holiday card was his chosen proxy for "caring." Not an enormous effort, to be sure, but not random.

Dunbar and his colleague Russell Hill (an anthropologist) discovered that about 25% of cards were sent to relatives, 65—70% to friends, and 5—10% to professional colleagues. Of interest, perhaps, but the study's most striking finding by far was one number: The average number of cards sent was 153.5: Round it to 150.

As soon as Dunbar and a number of other researchers began looking, the Dunbar number showed up everywhere:

- Hunter-gatherer clans tend to have about 150 members.

- From ancient Rome to 16th Century Spain to the Soviet Union to the allies in World War II, the typical size of an army company is 150 or so.

- Anabaptist sects split when they grow beyond 150 people; W.L. Gore & Associates (maker of Gore-Tex) does the same with its branches and production facilities.

- And now that we are in the age of social media, we learn that the average number of followers per Twitter user is about 200 (but over 40% of users have been dormant for the past year), while the median number of Facebook friends is also about 200 (but as many as half of Facebook pages are updated less than once a month).

150 is not the only number Dunbar's research has spawned. A consensus has emerged that there's more a Dunbar "scale" than a Dunbar "number:" Three to five people is the usual size of our innermost circle (think immediate family), 12 to 15 the next approximate grouping (the acid test here is often posed as "those whose death would be devastating"), and 50, the number of people we can be in more or less constant communication with, is the last stop before 150.

Finally, although the Dunbar number itself may appear somewhat arbitrary—why isn't it 100 or 250?—it turns out to be grounded in cognitive neurobiology based on primate studies: As the size of the neocortex expands relative to the rest of the brain, so does the maximum group size the species can accommodate. The causal explanation usually offered is that the number of inter-relationships between members of a group grows at a pace vastly disproportionate to the absolute number of individuals, and that as relationships proliferate it takes large jumps in mental processing power to keep track of everything. (A group of five has 10 bilateral relationships; a group of 20 has 190, a group of 50 has 1,225, and so forth.)

So what's all this got to do with the partnership structure? I think the link is quite straightforward.

The partnership governance model is premised on fundamental operating assumptions of widespread if not universal input, consensus, formal if not actual equality among members, and collaborative and distributed decision-making. But thousands of years of human history as crystallized into the Dunbar number research tell us there can be no such thing as an idealized partnership based on these principles, of indefinite scale. It's simply not within humans' cognitive capacity at this stage of evolution.

Now, you may be thinking that large-scale law firms have all implicitly recognized this reality by adopting governance mechanisms closer to the top-down, command-and-control end of the spectrum than the bottom-up, Athenian-democracy end. I would hasten to agree. They have had no choice.

The problem is they don't want to admit it too baldly and so maintain the pretense that they hew to a functioning partnership structure. If everyone at Large Firm X were winking and nodding and acquiescing in the pretense while understanding it had no teeth or substance, this might actually work out fine. A pretense universally subscribed to can prove highly functional.

That's not of course how people behave. Thinking that everyone would obediently subscribe to a fictional and imaginary governance model— "partnership"—with no one asserting the rights of consultation, voice, and voluntary consent that the model entails, is sheer fantasy.

In other words, "partners" will expect to be treated as partners. They will voice their opinions, assume a fair and serious-minded hearing, want to engage in extended discussion, and if all else fails will insist on asserting their prerogatives because they are an "owner"—and they are an owner, aren't they?

Here we run headfirst into the underappreciated distinction between facts and truth. Yes, partners are fractional owners of the partnership in *fact;* that's the common law of partnership 101. But in today's nation- or globe-spanning firms, the *truth* is that the rights and privileges partners' legal status as owners confers is far closer to that of shareholders in a public corporation: You can petition management for changes and vote on the composition of senior leadership, but if the firm chooses to pursue a course you irreconcilably disagree with, your only real choices are two: To hold your shares in mute acquiescence, or to sell.

Is it remotely conceivable law firms might begin to abandon the partnership model?

The days when such a shift might actually occur may be closer than you'd think. The 2016 IFLR1000 "Legal Market Trends" survey[13] found a striking disconnect between what partners in private practice believe about the

---

13   Conducted annually by Euromoney Trading Limited, the survey polls more than 1,500 of "the most experienced and knowledgeable individuals working in or around the legal industry worldwide," including CEO's, CFO's and COO's from a wide range of industries, senior and managing partners from leading law firms, and in-house counsel. Geographically, their representation ranges from New York, London, and Hong Kong to more than 120 other jurisdictions including Angola, Cambodia, and Myanmar.

partnership model and what in-house lawyers and corporate executives think. Specifically:

- "What do you think is the best business model for a law firm?"
  - Partners: 79% for partnership
  - Corporate executives and in-house: 52% for an equity-based corporate model

- "How do you see the structure of law firms changing in future?"
  - Partners: 62% see very few firms changing
  - Corporate executives and in-house: 51% believe movement to a corporate model is already in the cards

Partnership's Platonic Ideal

When you see two groups (as in the IFLR poll) who are fundamentally equivalent in terms of education, thoughtfulness, and upbringing, diverging like this in their views on a question, the simplest explanation is that one group is probably more emotionally invested on one side than the other. And so I think it is with law firm partners and corporate executives: Invoking the partnership model automatically and almost subconsciously invokes strong beliefs about camaraderie, mutuality, and sharing, felt more strongly by law firm partners. They are, after all, invested in the platform personally, and corporate executives are not.

Not for a moment do I mean to shortchange or underestimate the power of this mystique. Utterly to the contrary: Its power to cast spells that dissolve our rational faculties *is* the problem.

I devoutly believe that if we are to have any hope of maturing into the 21st Century as a profession and as an industry, we have to face our thoughtless and almost unconscious allegiance to the partnership model as an exercise in blind nostalgia, not a sober or serious way to grapple with new marketplace realities. As one of my favorite Managing Partners pointedly observed to an obstructionist colleague: "Nostalgia is not a strategy."

In short, we have to face partnership unblinkingly for what it is. Is there any there there?

One of the most ringing endorsements of partnership as an almost Platonic ideal recently came from someone in a better position to know than virtually anyone else in the world: Brad Karp, Chair of Paul Weiss.

At the time he delivered the address containing the excerpt which follows,[14] Paul Weiss's annual revenue was $1.11-billion, its operating income $543-million, and its profits per partner $4.09-million. The firm is a "single-tier" equity partnership (no non-equity partners) with 140 partners, more than 85% of whom are home-grown, and 800+ counsel, associates, and staff attorneys. More than 80% of Paul Weiss lawyers are based in New York with another 10% in Washington (the remainder are in Wilmington, Toronto, London, Beijing, Hong Kong, and Tokyo).

Paul Weiss presents a textbook case of the ingredients required for a true partnership:

- A limited number of partners, preferably (as with Paul Weiss) less than the Dunbar ceiling;

- Mostly in a single office location (80%);

- With a long history of working together (85% lifers).

Another ideal example is Slaughter and May, "the most magical of the Magic Circle firms." For nearly 130 years it has operated out of a single stronghold in London (barring a few partners in Hong Kong) and over 80% of its 120 or so partners are lifers; about three out of five have been with the firm over 20 years, and no lateral has ever entered as a partner. In the firm's upstairs dining room at its Bunhill Row headquarters, each partner has a cubbyhole for their napkin.[15]

The mystique such a partnership-as-ideal still holds is surely reinforced by this and other such potent and romantic images as the "partners' desk," a single piece of furniture with space for two people to work opposite each other.

---

14   Brad Karp, Chair of the Firm, Paul Weiss, Keynote Address at the Bloomberg *Business of Law Summit,* (New York: June 2016)

15   James Ashton, *Chris Saul Interview: Slaughter and May purrs like a Porsche but that doesn't mean we're run by Buff and Bertie,* The Independent (November 23, 2014): at http://www.independent.co.uk/news/people/profiles/chris-saul-interview-slaughter-and-may-purrs-like-a-porsche-but-that-doesn-t-mean-we-re-run-by-buffy-9878727.html

But back to Paul Weiss:

Partner compensation there follows a modified lockstep system where the ratio of highest to lowest paid partner is ~4:1. More than 90% of partners are on the straight modified lockstep system, with 2% of annual firm revenue set aside in a bonus pool for outstanding performance.

In other words, an extraordinarily successful firm. Brad's thoughts on partnership:

> Let me now focus on the importance of culture, values, and partnership. To me, business and culture are inextricably intertwined: *Nothing* is more important to a law firm's continued success than its culture, its values, and a true sense of partnership.
>
> Money is no substitute for enjoying what you do and doing it in a supportive, nurturing, and professional environment, surrounded by brilliant colleagues you like and trust implicitly. The importance of culture and partnership has never been greater; culture and partnership are tested most in times of great uncertainty.
>
> The firms that have struggled most have been those facing crises of culture; too many firms have recently disintegrated because of a lack of cohesion, silo'ed partners and practices, unchecked greed, the rise of divisive, power-hungry factions, and sharp elbows.
>
> Clients detest even the slightest whiff of an aroma of internal bickering.

How hard could this be? you may be thinking. Shouldn't these observations be self-evident to anyone with a bit of experience in Law Land who thinks about it seriously for a moment?

Now, Gentle Reader, I must confess I have struggled with this intersection of magical words—namely, what people as insightful as Brad Karp are *truly* driving at when they talk about "culture, values, and partnership"—harder and for longer than I will admit to you.

The first obstacle I encountered is straightforward enough: Ninety-nine out of 100 law firms talk about how their "collaborative" and "collegial" "culture" sets them apart (and the 100th is probably just being ornery—wait until they get a new marketing director, or managing partner). If everyone claims to be distinctive in exactly the same way, we need to think harder about who we all are, or who each of us is.

On the other hand, everybody wants to achieve what Paul Weiss has, and if Brad-Karp-no-less is telling us that "*nothing*" is more important to that success than culture &c., should we really be surprised if every firm and its cousins lay claim to that very thing?

The second obstacle I found myself wrestling with under the gnarly heading of culture is this: Remind me exactly why clients should care about your firm's culture? Isn't that a benefit, if it's a benefit to anyone, to the lawyers and professionals who work at your firm? Do consumers probe the corporate cultures of, say, Audi, BMW, and Lexus before selecting their next car?

On the other hand, clients manifestly appreciate and benefit from being served by professionals who collaborate nicely together, fluidly deliver the work to the most qualified individual in the firm regardless of ego or self-interest, and who perform as a well-oiled team. And, the car analogy isn't quite fair since the automotive manufacturer's product is, well, an automobile, and a law firm's product (service) is interaction with its lawyers. Presumably clients can roughly assess how a firm's lawyers get along together but what goes on in the BMW executive suite is not of the least moment whatever.

But this won't do, either. It merely pushes the question back one level.

Here's what I mean:

- If we know that essentially every firm asserts that it cares about, promotes, and lives the "culture, values, and partnership" Brad Karp is talking about;

- But we also know for a fact that can't be true because (a) vanishingly few firms actually perform as Paul Weiss has; and (b) clients experience demeaning treatment at the hands of arrogant lawyers every day (the "whiff of an aroma of internal bickering");

- Then what *really* separates firms who walk the culture walk from those who just talk the culture talk?

This finally brought me to a focus on the notion of symmetry within a partnership. A strong and vibrant partnership possesses, strengthens, and celebrates symmetry at its core: Individual members benefit, thrive, and prosper only as, and as much as, the partnership itself does so. Stronger and more capable individual members empower a stronger and more capable partnership, and vice versa.

Alternative ways of expressing this same value would invoke notions of mutuality, reciprocity, and, at the core, stewardship. Partners recognize their standing as members entails expectations, responsibilities, and mutual obligations to other members and to the institution itself. Similarly, the organization imposes its own standards, flexible and humane in the short run but rigorous and non-negotiable in the long run, of citizenship, decency, and high performance.[16]

Contrast this model of reciprocity and symmetry with what one sees all too often in Law Land: Partners who treat the organization as a sort of ad hoc co-op, helpful in provisioning some basic services and tools useful for their practice, such as an office, a business card, a bit of IT, and a pool of more or less willing and more or less available associates, but otherwise fungible with any number of other firms in town: A "hotel for lawyers," you might call it. Check in, check out, at your pleasure, loyalty quotient negotiable.

This model pushes asymmetry to the extreme, elevating the self-interest of the individual over that of the firm to a fault. But simple observation and experience teach that for many lawyers today, this is not asymmetry as hell but asymmetry as heaven—or at least as job security in a heartless world, behind the invincible shield of one's portable practice.

---

16   It's a safe bet Brad Karp would agree: At the same Bloomberg *Business of Law* Summit, he was asked how he dealt with partners who indulged in some form of anti-social conduct. He said he would talk to them immediately and make it clear their behavior was inexcusable. "And how do you enforce that?" he was asked. His answer in full was: "I sit on the compensation committee."

Who can blame people? you may be asking. After all, firms haven't exactly demonstrated overflowing measures of loyalty to partners, lately, have they? Consider how the AmLaw 200 firms have been performing over the past decade (2005—2015),[17] and how parsimonious they've been with the ranks of the equity compared to the change in the dollars coming in the door:

- Total revenue has grown from $59.521-billion to $100.358-billion, or 69.4% (a compound annual growth rate of 5.41%);

- The average firm's revenue grew from $297.6-million to $501.8-million (virtually identical growth rates, for tautological arithmetic reasons);

- The number of lawyers went from 94,214 (a firm average of 471) to 122,829 (a firm average of 614), or total growth of 30.0% and a CAGR of 2.69%; but

- The number of equity partners rose only from 26,755 (a firm average of 134) to 29,834 (a firm average of 149) or 11.5% overall, yielding a CAGR of 1.09%.

If you're wondering how all this additional work gets performed, I have two words for you: Non-equity partners. Their ranks have grown from 10,780 to 21,270, or 97.3%. Expressed differently, for every $1.00 AmLaw 200 firms collected ten years ago they're now collecting $1.69, but for every 100 non-equity partners they had ten years ago they now have 197 and for every 100 equity partners 10 years ago there are now 111.

You might excuse this as understandable in the wake of the Great Financial Reset of 2007—2008, but (a) that ought to be pretty far in our collective rear-view mirrors' by now; and (b) the equity-compression phenomenon shows no sign of abating. To the contrary, the 2016 AmLaw 100 collectively *shrank* the ranks of equity partners by -0.6% vs. the previous year, and for the AmLaw Second Hundred the story was even worse: Equity headcount dropped -2.0%. This trend is not your friend. Indeed, figures like these should call to mind the teaching about the camel and the eye of a needle.

---

17   *The American Lawyer's* "AmLaw 200" for 2005 and 2015.

It long since ceased to surprise that de-equitization's are everywhere, or that people openly remark, oblivious to the macabre, that to make equity partner "I'm just waiting for someone to die." My greater fear by far is that the true meaning of the word "partner" itself seems to have been traduced. Benjamin Cardozo's ringing call defining the standards expected of partners sounds quaint in more ways than linguistically. Have you heard anyone lately insist that in their dealings with one another partners should be "held to something stricter than the morals of the market place. Not honesty alone, but the punctilio of an honor the most sensitive is then the standard of behavior."[18]

Our legal, professional-responsibility, and institutional structures surrounding the rights and responsibilities that come with the title "partner," at least in the law firm context, also skew heavily towards elevating the self-interest of the individual over the well-being of the firm. For starters, the ABA's Model Rules of Professional Conduct prohibit any agreement that "restricts the right of a lawyer to practice after termination of the relationship [with a firm.]" (Model Rule §5.6.) Non-competes may be enforceable against some other less privileged professionals, but not against us.[19]

The lateral partner talent market has never been more liquid and active, and high-profile moves can have cumulative repercussions far more consequential than providing a topic for the day's gossip. I pursue this in much more depth in Chapter III, "Talent and Free Agency Win," but for now it suffices to note that unfettered lateral partner mobility presupposes a fairly ragged if not tattered state of firm loyalty.

---

18   *Meinhard v. Salmon*, 249 N.Y. 458, 164 N.E 545 (1928).

19   The strong consensus of dispassionate labor market economic analysis is that non-competes impose substantial unjustifiable costs on workers, customers, and the economy in general. (This is setting aside legitimate reasons firms may have for protecting trade secrets, a concern which can be addressed in far more targeted ways with minimal collateral damage.) *See, e.g.* Gilson, Ronald J. 1999. "The Legal Infrastructure of High Technology Industrial Districts: Silicon Valley, Route 128, and Covenants Not to Compete." New York University Law Review 74 (3): 575–629, which argues that one reason among many others Massachusetts lost out to California in the high tech talent race was that Massachusetts state law enforced non-competes and California prohibited them.

However, my point has nothing to do with the desirability or lack thereof of non-competes in the economy writ large; it has to do with lawyers' exempting themselves from a widespread practice.

And yet: Have I forgotten so quickly Brad Karp's ringing defense of the power and the virtues of partnership? How do we square this circle?

Actually, we just have to reflect on some additional remarks of Brad's contained in the same Bloomberg *Big Law Summit* keynote I quoted earlier. Consider:

> We are operating in in a period of unprecedented turbulence, instability, and fragility. ...
>
> We have seen many firms teeter under the twin pressures of overcapacity and under demand. We have seen the exodus of key partners from elite law firms, and an unprecedented shuffling of clients between the haves and the have-nots. The gap between the elite firms and the next tier is widening every year. We have watched the gradual erosion of both partner loyalty and client loyalty. Many firms have lost their footing. ...
>
> The legal world has become increasingly punitive and unforgiving.

Harsh? I'd call it realistic.

The attentive reader will recall I noted somewhat parenthetically that almost any rational firm would be thrilled to emulate Paul Weiss's performance. Be careful what you wish for.

Partnerships in name only

Here's what I mean: I have profound reservations about whether any but the most high-performing of firms—the New York and London super-elite, as well as a select handful of highly focused boutiques (often with a single office)—can actually live up to the rigorous and demanding principles, standards of behavior, and non-negotiable "firm-first" orientation that a lived and vibrant partnership model necessarily entails.[20]

---

20   Somewhat arbitrarily but since it's (a) highly indicative of the kinds of firms I'm describing here, and also (b) a matter of public record [this list is drawn from the May 2016 edition of *The American Lawyer* (at p. 45)], here are the AmLaw 100 firms with single-tier, equity-only, partnerships: Arnold & Porter, Ballard Spahr, Cleary, Covington, Cravath, Davis Polk, Debevoise, Paul Weiss, Ropes & Gray, Schulte, Simpson Thacher, Skadden, Steptoe, Sullivan & Cromwell, Wachtell, Wilmer, Williams & Connolly, and Willkie Farr.

Where does that leave the other 90%+ of law firms nominally structured as "partnerships?" I will, with relief, leave you to draw your own conclusions, but make no mistake: Creating and *sustaining* a partnership that means what it says is hard. Doubt me? In that case, Brad Karp again:

> We need to have the fortitude and the confidence to turn away clients and matters that are not strategic, and to minimize the time we spend handling one-off clients that are not strategic.
>
> Perhaps no aspect of our strategy has been more critical to our success than our laser-like focus on investing in our core practice strengths and steering clear of non-core practice areas and non-core jurisdictions. ... We have resisted the temptation to dabble in non-core or exotic practices or to open new offices in far-flung jurisdictions around the world in search of increased revenue.
>
> There is *nothing* strategic about one-off clients and one-off matters. To a law firm leader, there is nothing more frustrating than hearing a client described within the firm as a corporate client or a litigation client; law firms need to tackle this challenge head-on.

Are you really prepared to do this at your firm? Because this is what being a true partnership, and not one in name only, requires:

- Turning away clients whose work is not aligned with the firm's strategic purpose;

- Cutting to a bare minimum time spent on (and revenue derived from...) one-off clients;

- Saying no, and no again, and no again, to partners eager to expand the firm's practice focus or office base because they spy an opportunity for additional revenue (accruing to them, we can speculate without fear of contradiction); and

- Expunging the vocabulary of client "ownership" from the firm's lexicon—clients are not owned by partners, by offices, by practice groups, or by any entity whatsoever other than the firm itself.

If the leaders of firms are not prepared to enforce these standards of conduct, or the partners elevate their self-interest above these principles (by, not to be oblique about it, leaving), then firms are at liberty to be organized as partnerships in legal form, but one must ask whether they aren't partnerships in name only? Haven't they drained the vitality out of the partnership ideal and retained only the hollow vessel?

Perhaps this line of thinking helps explain the universality and durability of the partnership model in Law Land: People know in their hearts there are core virtues of immense value in the Platonic ideal of partnership, but they fall short of living it in their daily lives and through their actual firms.

Call this far-fetched if you wish, but the story of why the Israelites, in the Exodus from Egypt, created a golden calf to worship when Moses left them and stayed up on the mountain for a while, has long baffled me. After all, the Israelites knew about the Real Thing; why create a shallow and false simulacrum instead?

I have to wonder whether this same psychological dynamic—recognizing the value of the *authentic* but falling short of what it demands in terms of your day to day behavior in practice—lies at the heart of explaining why countless law firms adopt the partnership form in name only.

A generous interpretation would be that everyone had the right instincts and recognized the value of what they had seen, been told about, and were aspiring to (the Ten Commandments and the Covenant, in Scripture; the lived values Brad Karp is committed to, in Law Land), but that they yielded to temptation ("proclaiming a festival, ...sitting down to eat and drink, and rising up to revel") when they realized they were in at least short-term control.[21]

True partnership is *hard*. It requires autonomy-seeking Type A's to believe, and live out the belief, that their individual relationship with the firm entails bilateral obligations—meaning membership entails behavioral, attitudinal, and performance expectations with teeth—and it demands one choose the long run over the short run, investment for the future over consumption this fiscal year, and collaboration over control.

---

21   *Exodus* 32.

"Eating and drinking, and rising up to revel"—compared to being called upon to sacrifice one's first-born? *Seriously?*

Fortunately, living out a true partnership isn't as existentially challenging as that, but it can be a very serious business indeed. When Tony Angel was head of Linklaters and was putting the firm through what could delicately be called a talent upgrade, he remarked by way of explanation, "There is no such thing as a tolerant lockstep."

Above all, true partnership embodies subscribing to a belief in stewardship: The essential motivating conviction that one has stepped into an organization built in part by others who came before and that one's obligation, heart and head, is to leave the firm better than one found it. This is why the long run matters.

Ethics (properly understood) and "career planning"

An objection will be raised—you may be doing so as we speak—that the partnership form is indispensable to maintaining professional ethical standards, ensuring consensus across a spectrum of autonomy-seeking Type A personalities, and focusing organizational verve and energy against agreed strategic objectives.

But precisely because the partnership form is essentially universal, we actually have no empirical evidence to back up these assertions. In other words, we don't know, and this recitation of faith-based beliefs doesn't address, how the world might look different if in fact the world were different. Occasionally I point out that essentially every moderately sophisticated enterprise in the economy outside Law Land has adopted the corporate form, but this anodyne observation is usually met with expressions indicating anyone who could say that must be willfully ignorant of the peculiar mores essential to lawyers' healthy functioning.

Whenever I've gone beyond that and questioned out loud whether partnership still makes any sense for the vast majority of firms, it doesn't do justice to the reactions I've encountered to call them "skeptical:" They go far beyond that familiar territory into a different planetary orbit altogether, somewhere between disbelief and flat incomprehension. So deeply rooted is the assumption that law firms simply *are* partnerships that the topic is just not open for discussion.

This attitude is fantastically ahistorical.

It also misconstrues, if I may be so bold, the principles behind what constitutes a truly "conservative" approach to life, society, and its institutions—which I mention only because those espousing would insist their point of view reflects and is justified by their preferring a conservative approach. But words matter, and when it comes to seeking the original principles animating the conservative worldview, we have few more qualified spokesmen than Edmund Burke (1729—1797):

> His was a pragmatic approach above all else. What impressed him about political institutions was not their origins in speculative theories, but their capacity, or failure, to meet the real needs of men living in a political community... Always, Burke is responding to the events of his time.[22]

Burke expresses this core belief just a few pages into his magnum opus, *Reflections on the Revolution in France* (1789):

> Circumstances (which with some gentlemen pass for nothing) give in reality to every political principle its distinguishing color and discriminating effect. The circumstances are what render every civil and political scheme beneficial or noxious to mankind.[23]

In other words, partnership as an organizational form for law firms should not be venerated as some icon handed down from our wise predecessors,

---

22   Leslie Mitchell (Fellow in Modern History, University College, Oxford) in the preface to Edmund Burke's *Reflections on the Revolution in France* (1790) (Oxford World Classics edition: Oxford University Press 2009) at i.

23   Burke's *Reflections (id.)*, at 8.

One of the most prominent consequences of Burke's belief in the primacy of circumstance was that his views on the American Revolution (pro) were directly opposite his views on the French Revolution (con), despite their surface similarities. At the risk of doing violence to the subtlety of his thinking, he favored the American colonists' efforts as true to vindicating the rights of the colonists and "conserving" traditional institutions and traditions against British usurpation, but thought the French revolution "a digest of anarchy" aimed at displacing traditional French institutions and traditions and building a new society from the ground up.

which we might dispense with at our peril. It should only be viewed through the lens of how it's serving today's "real needs" and whether current circumstances render it "beneficial or noxious."

So how does the partnership form measure up in the 21st Century?

What we do know is that the vast majority of other sophisticated B2B professional service firms are organized in the corporate form and seem to have found it empowering. The other professional service firms I'm referring to include of course the Big Four accounting firms; consultancies such as McKinsey, Bain, and BCG; communications agencies such as Omnicom and Publicis; and of course the global and boutique investment banks and private equity houses.

It's possible we're the only ones who are right and they're all wrong, but one must at the least have the intellectual integrity to take pause.

Here let us step back and stipulate for argument's sake that a primary goal of a business enterprise is to define, articulate, and pursue a distinctive strategy. In that light, the question whether the partnership form or the corporate firm is more fit for purpose can be rephrased to ask, which is more likely to advance the goals of the firm's strategy?

If nothing else, strategy requires making choices and saying no. (Recall Brad Karp's non-negotiable views on one-off clients and one-off matters.) What's the primary obstacle, in a law firm, to making and sticking with choices? We all know the answer: Partners who object, and who insist their objection carries weight because, after all, they're an owner. Here I must quote a wise managing partner of my acquaintance who requests anonymity:

> *Be careful not to confuse the career aspirations and personal*
> *preferences of the current incumbent owners with the mission of*
> *the organization. That is not strategy—it is career planning at best,*
> and a bunch of lawyers simply sharing overhead disguised as an
> enterprise with purpose at worst [my emphasis].

Our friend has nailed an inconvenient truth: An extraordinary number of law firms are managed, de facto if not de jure, to serve the short-term career preferences of the partners first and last.

In some ways, one must empathize with law firm managing partners and executive committees: It's rational on their part to only care (really care) about how the firm fares so long as they're around, and a cursory glance at demographics tells you for most any firm you pick at random that will not be terribly long—certainly not a lifetime, or even much of a meaningful span in a career.

George Bernard Shaw may have been harsh but he put his finger on what happens next: "Old men are dangerous: It doesn't matter to them what is going to happen to the world."[24]

The corporate form has another powerful advantage: The flexibility to design and implement long-term compensation packages tying the individual's well-being to that of the firm, even after people depart: Long-term incentive compensation, stock options, restricted stock, a variety of forms of deferred compensation, earn-outs, etc., all make it in the self-interest of high-level employees that the corporation thrive after their departure or, at the very least, remain a going concern.

Law firm partners, by contrast?

The point is self-evident and may seem of slender import, but if you believe as do I that incentives matter, reflect for a moment on how behavior might differ *while one is working at the firm* if you knew your long-run self-interest depended on the firm's success in future.

Fragility and its opposite

Turning from promoting dysfunctional mental models to embedding suboptimal financial characteristics, you might think that lawyers, of all professionals, would have chosen a default organizational structure for their firms that is tax-efficient. You might think they'd choose a form that rewards longevity and continuity, or that frees them from an

---

24   Words of the 88-year-old character Captain Shotover in the play *Heartbreak House.*

expectation that they'll need to contribute essentially permanent capital to their firms out of their own pockets (at least as long as they choose to remain associated with the firm). You might imagine they'd choose a form that would enable them to reward senior business professionals with a compensation package competitive with what's found in every other industry in the economy.

Yes, you might imagine.

Yet the partnership form frustrates every one of these sensible objectives.

Distributing all compensation in the form of ordinary income is about as tax-inefficient as you can get, yet this is definitional to how partnerships function.

Since partners pay individual income taxes on all profits of the partnership—whether or not they're actually distributed and received—leaving "retained earnings" on the partnership's books for future investment and growth is so costly and unattractive to the individual members that it simply never happens in reality.

In order for the partnership as an operating economic entity to have any permanent capital—beyond, say, a working capital line of credit drawn down at the beginning of the fiscal year and normally repaid within 60 to 90 days—the all but universal method of raising capital is, as a droll managing partner of our acquaintance says, "passing the hat among friends." In other words, requiring partner capital contributions.

Yes, law firms can and do obtain term loans from banks and other forms of longer-dated debt (and a number countable on the fingers of one hand have actually placed debt issues into the private markets, most notoriously including the late unlamented Dewey & LeBoeuf's $125-million offering purchased by insurance companies).

But bank debt has acquired a bad name in law firm management circles, for logical and understandable reasons, not the least being the loan covenants it invariably comes with, including security interests in tangible collateral and accounts receivable, limitations or bans on secondary financing, and even quasi-structural restrictions such as a requirement that a certain minimum number of partners remain active in the firm or that quarterly revenue not drop below specified minimums.

These covenants have teeth and the consequences of violating them can be dire, up to and including the death of the firm. Famous dissolutions including Brobeck, Coudert Bros., Heller, Howrey, Shea & Gould, and Thacher Proffitt all came about when banks turned out the lights. Certainly these firms all were in profound financial difficulty with or without bank debt, but it was the banks who turned off the life support of cash. Remember that it doesn't matter how much money is coming in the door or how much your P&L says is dropping to the bottom line; when cash goes negative, it's lights out.[25]

We cannot leave this section without recounting the reverse-O. Henry story of the last days of Finley Kumble, a New York-based firm variously described as "a moon shot," "a Ponzi scheme," "a house of horrors," and "Harvey Myerson's version of the go-go 80's" that imploded on Christmas Eve in 1987, having grown to 700 lawyers and then the fourth largest law firm in the country (at its peak it was the second largest behind only Baker & McKenzie). The proximate cause of death? The firm's bank refused to extend its line of credit to cover Christmas bonuses for the staff. Sure, Finley Kumble was an outlier extraordinaire, but it wasn't the last. One has to ask, What have we learned?

What these seemingly innocent and quotidian financial and accounting implications of the partnership form have in common is that they all but compel rational self-interested actors to put the short run first:

- to extract maximum economic value out of the firm by the end of each and every fiscal year,

- to dismiss any notion of keeping retained earnings on the firm's balance sheet, investing in R&D, or placing measured (but nonzero) economic bets on new initiatives,

- and to be prepared to renegotiate (or abandon) one's position in the firm if a decision or a few go against one's preferences.

---

25   The hoary Wall Street maxim has it right: "Revenue is vanity, profit is sanity, but cash is king."

After all, the vast majority of partners have nothing to lose by walking out, save perhaps a bit of undistributed draw—which can be salvaged by timing one's departure with a jot more discretion and calculation. Law firms, in short, are fragile.

Thanks to Professor Nassim Nicholas Taleb,[26] the concept of antifragility has entered our lexicon; it refers to systems that, in response to shocks, mistakes, faults, volatility, and other adverse developments, *increase* in their ability to withstand the stress rather than being compromised and weakened by it. It's akin to resilience, but more. Resilient systems recover gracefully from failure; antifragile systems emerge stronger than ever.

If market conditions are increasingly challenging and hostile to law firms in their classic operational form, a dose of antifragility would be in order. I am not positing that there are no such law firms—that's often an empirical question, and one doesn't know in advance whether fire will consume the firm or temper and toughen it. I am however positing that structurally law firms are more subject to partners' "me first" instincts trumping the "firm first" obligation one has when one joins an organization.

The most toxic expression of the "me" before "firm" mindset is partner desertion—cost-free to the individuals involved but a dynamic which can quickly escalate into a crisis for the firm.

A run on the bank

This untethered liberty to walk out the door at a whiff of real or perceived unpleasantness can quickly metastasize into a vicious and essentially unstoppable pattern of partners losing faith in a firm—for any reason or for no reason. The phenomenon is hardly limited to Law Land, as it invokes the classic economic game-theory dilemma of the "collective action problem," but this only underscores its power.

The mechanism and consequences are masterfully spelled out by Mervyn King in *The End of Alchemy* when he discusses the genesis of the global

---

26   Most prominently in *Antifragile: Things that gain from Disorder,* (Random House: New York) 2012.

financial crisis of 2007. King should know; he was governor of the Bank of England from 2003 to 2013.[27]

In *Alchemy* (at pp. 114-115) he describes the mechanism of the vortex of destruction by invoking Walter Bagehot's description of how the phenomenon of a run on the bank develops, taken from Bagehot's 1873 classic, *Lombard Street: A Description of the Money Market* (Henry S. King and Co., London) at p. 49:

> At first, incipient panic amounts to a kind of vague conversation: Is A. B. still as good as he used to be? Has not C.D. lost money? and a thousand such questions. A hundred people are talked about, and a thousand think, 'Am I talked about, or am I not?' 'Is my credit as good as it used to be, or is it less?' And every day, as a panic grows, this floating suspicion becomes both more intense and more diffused; it attacks more person; and attacks them all more virulently than at first.

All men of experience, therefore, try to 'strengthen themselves,' as it is called, in the early stage of a panic; they borrow money while they can; they come to their banker and offer bills for discount, which commonly they would not have offered for days or weeks to come. And if the merchant be a regular customer, a banker does not like to refuse, because if he does he will be said, or may be said, to be in want of money, and so may attract the panic to himself.

• • •

The call of the Platonic ideal is a powerful one indeed. But looking honestly, it's the rarest of firms that does, or even can, live it. The short run seduces almost every time.

Wouldn't we be immensely better off, invoking Plato, to venture out of the cave and take an honest look at the partnership form?

---

27   King is now Baron King of Lothbury, a Knight of the Garter, and a professor at both New York University and the London School of Economics.

Shed your skepticism, step back from the enchantment of the mystique, engage your critical and analytic faculties, and analyze whether partnership remains "fit for purpose."

Because until we do this, the dynamic of latent centrifugal forces ready to spin up inside a firm like a dormant virus, will remain with us, ready to strike at a moment of weakened resistance. All we require is the courage to take a hard look.

"I'm kind of stupefied by the numbers. They're beyond alarming. … Clearly we are in a crisis situation."

—Major League Baseball executive
Sandy Alderson, reacting to news that the Texas Rangers
had signedshortstop Alex Rodriguez to a 10-year, $252-million
contract (in December 2000).

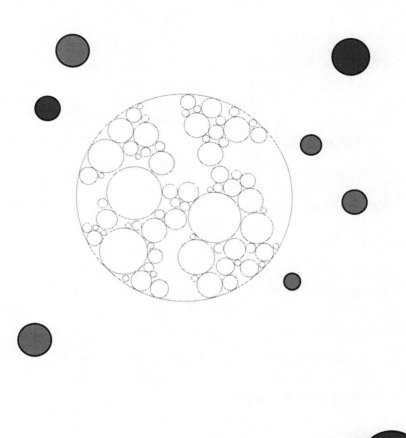

Talent and Free Agency Win

Law firms operate in a ~~war~~ market for talent. If you visualize a law firm within the simplest possible Econ 101 model, clients are a firm's demand and lawyers are its supply. Any firm is only as good as its lawyers.

It turns out that we can learn a fair amount from economic and management literature about the characteristics of talent markets— including the particular type of talent market law firms operate in. Our market for the labor of lawyers has several characteristics:

- One can assume without fear of doing great violence to reality that the allocation of talent (innate ability as a lawyer) roughly resembles a bell curve, or a "normal" distribution. Relatively few lawyers are exceedingly bad or utterly superb; the vast majority by far are average, certainly more than "good enough" almost all of the time.

- Performance, or quality of analysis and work product as a lawyer, is reasonably transparent and becomes self-evident over time. Certainly over the span of a few years or more, objective observers will fairly readily agree on who qualifies for the A Team, the B Team, and so forth.

- To the extent that pure quality is subjective or intangible and elusive of definition, reputation provides a readily available and not irrational substitute. Reputations are sticky, self-reinforcing, and self-perpetuating.

- If 95 or 97 or 99+% of lawyers are "good enough" for clients "most of the time," it remains the case that sometimes clients demand nothing less than the A++ players.

If these constitute a reasonable description of the dynamics of the lawyer talent market, it's not difficult to predict how the market will, left to its own devices, want to evolve. It will migrate towards a "power curve," or exponential, distribution of income. Natural constraints limit how extreme this can become in the case of lawyers but let's explore how such markets work.

The economics of talent markets

Two talent markets that are conceptually congruent to ours are those for professional sports stars and entertainment celebrities. It's for a reason that I opened this chapter with a quote about what remains, over 15 years later, one of the most notorious sports contracts of all time: How that played out is recounted in full below; suffice to say, better for "A-Rod" than for the teams paying his salary.[28]

On the entertainment front, we have the opposite outcome, or at least the opposite judgment exercised by the "signing" entity: The legendary rock & roll impresario Ahmet Ertegun (1923—2006), who in his long career founded Atlantic Records on West 56th Street in New York with $10,000 borrowed from his dentist, and went on to sign artists such as Otis Redding, Aretha Franklin, Led Zeppelin, Crosby, Stills & Nash, and, most famously, The Rolling Stones (when their contract with Decca Records was up), chose to walk away from the Stones when his business judgment told him he should.

To provide perspective on how emotionally difficult this decision must have been, consider not only that he would be abandoning what was by far Atlantic's most celebrated band, but Ertegun was close personal friends with Mick Jagger. (Ertegun, a Stones fan to the end, died at age 83 after lapsing into a coma when he fell and hit his head—attending a Stones concert.)

What drove Ertegun's decision? At the end of a Stones' contract with Atlantic, Virgin Records offered the band what Ertegun thought was an

---

28   As ESPN reported on the 15th anniversary of the contract's signing, "the numbers were staggering on December 11, 2000, and they remain formidable a decade and a half [later]." (http://espn.go.com/mlb/story/_/id/14330504/alex-rodriguez-252-million-contract-texas-rangers-remains-landmark-15th-anniversary) The Rangers held on to A-Rod for only three seasons before they traded him to the Yankees to get out from under what had become an enormous financial albatross—A'Rod's average annual $25.2-million salary with the Rangers exceeded the entire payroll of three other teams in 2000 (The Milwaukee Brewers, Kansas City Royals, and Minnesota Twins) and was 11 times that of the average MLB player.

But A-Rod's enormous compensation could, economically, be justified if it boosted the Rangers' performance and stadium attendance sufficiently. This is where the story becomes instructive: With the Rangers, A-Rod did what he was hired to do, leading the American League in home runs each year, in the top two players in total bases and the top three in RBI's, winning an all-league MVP. But it did the team no good: they finished dead last in the American League West division all three years with A-Rod, whereas during the previous three years they'd actually won two division titles and over the subsequent three years they finished third every year. Nor did their attendance budge.

Bottom line: A-Rod collected the entire present discounted value of his talents (and perhaps more); there was nothing left over for the team.

impossibly lucrative deal. Ertegun told Jagger he couldn't match the offer and let the Stones go. He didn't see how there would be anything left over for Atlantic if it matched what Virgin was prepared to pay; the band would appropriate all the profit to itself. Lore has it that Ertegun was right; but whether he was right or wrong *in fact* in this particular case is not material to my point: Clearly there is some price at which acquiring talent is irrational for the firm—even if the talent is The Rolling Stones and you're the genius impresario Ahmet Ertegun.

Other markets have similar characteristics, some even more pronounced. After all, natural physical and human laws limit the amount of revenue A-Rod or the Stones can conceivably generate for their organizations: There are only 162 games during the regularly scheduled baseball season and the Stones have to keep producing albums and touring. If we relax those constraints and assume the marginal cost of an additional unit of production/service is essentially zero for the "owner" of the talent, more extreme outcomes result.

Two examples are "Author Rank" on Amazon and investment money managers. Amazon doesn't publish statistics on exactly how many book sales are required to achieve what level of Author Rank, but plausible estimates from people who've studied the topic produce distributions like this[29]:

Sales rank 50,000 to 100,000 — one book per day
Sales rank 10,000 to 50,000 — 3 to 15 books per day
Sales rank 5,500 to 10,000 — 15 to 30 books per day
Sales rank 3,000 to 5,500 — 30 to 50 books per day
Sales rank 500 to 3,000 — 50 to 200 books per day
Sales rank 350 to 500 — 200 to 300 books per day
Sales rank 100 to 350 — 300 to 500 books per day
Sales rank 35 to 100 — 500 to 800 books per day
Sales rank 10 to 35 — 800 to 2,000 books per day
Sales rank 5 to 10 — 2,000 to 3,500 books per day
Sales rank 1 to 5 — 3,500+ books per day
Sales rank 1: over 10,000 books per day

You can imagine what this looks like graphically, and it's a classic power curve distribution:

---

29   https://kdp.amazon.com/community/message.jspa?messageID=969951

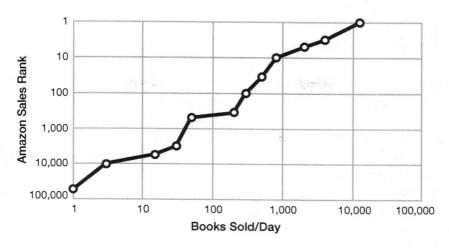

Amazon Daily Book Sales vs. Sales Rank

Similarly with investment money managers: The top handful of hedge fund Masters of the Universe in Greenwich, Connecticut, can each earn billions of dollars a year, while a rank and file portfolio analyst at (say) Vanguard or Fidelity may earn an income barely qualifying them for the upper middle class—certainly if they want to live in Greenwich or Manhattan.

Had we all been paying attention, we might have seen this coming back in 1981 when Sherwin Rosen, an economics professor at the University of Chicago, published a prescient and diminutive 12-page article, *The Economics of Superstars.*[30] He opens straightforwardly enough:

> The phenomenon of Superstars, wherein relatively small numbers of people earn enormous amounts of money and dominate the activities in which they engage seems to be increasingly important in the modern world.[31]

He notes that only about 200 full-time comedians could earn a living in the US at the time, that full-time classical music soloists might number not many more, and that almost all sales of elementary economics textbooks were captured by just a few best-sellers.

---

30   American Economic Review, Volume 71, Issue 5 (Dec. 1981) at 845-858: http://home.uchicago.edu/~vlima/courses/econ201/Superstars.pdf

31   Id. at 845.

What might cause a market to fall into this type of anomalous behavior? (I use the term "anomalous" in its rather formal sense, meaning atypical, abnormal, or out of the ordinary—as markets go—not in the sense of inexplicable or baffling.)

Certainly the most powerful driver of this kind of winner-take-most market is the phenomenon of "imperfect substitution," the economic-ese label for those rare markets which don't adhere to the conventional pattern where buyers' preferences can encompass lower quality offerings in exchange for their being offered at a lower price.   Instead, these markets adamantly reject the standard price/quality tradeoff continuum; here, buyers still perceive quality differences between performers, but almost no matter how small they're nevertheless sufficient to make the lesser-quality alternatives unacceptable at almost any price.   If you want to hear Yo-Yo Ma, the finest orchestras' lead cellists are no substitute.

Rosen describes this phenomenon with a combination of jargon and plain English:

> Lesser talent is often a poor substitute for greater talent. The worse it is the larger the sustainable rent accruing to higher quality sellers because demand for the better sellers increases more than proportionately; hearing a succession of mediocre singers does not add up to a single outstanding performance. If a surgeon is 10% more successful in saving lives than his fellows, most people would be willing to pay more than a 10% premium for his services. A company involved in a $30-million law suit is rash to scrimp on the legal talent it engages [$30-million in 1981 is about $125-million in 2016].[32]

Like every market worth talking about, this one is also bilateral, and it turns out considering not just disparate talent of sellers but motivating influences on preferences by buyers strongly reinforces the effects of imperfect substitution and rewards superstars even more.   You can see

---

32   Id at 846. Alfred Marshall made the same point in 1947 in his *Principles of Economics* (8th ed. New York: MacMillan) at 685-86:

> [A few] barristers command very high fees, for a rich client whose reputation, or fortune, or both, are at stake will scarcely count any price too high to secure the services of the best man he can get.

this by thinking for a moment about the value of that $30-million/$125-million lawsuit to the client.

Start by considering the extreme case where the lawsuit has nuisance value: No one is going to hire top-drawer talent at $1,000 or £1,000/hour and up to defend such a suit. But at some threshold level of value—monetary, reputational, principled, and otherwise—hiring the best that Gibson Dunn, Kirkland, Paul Weiss, or [others among the usual suspects] can offer becomes justified. Now we're in territory where second best simply will not do.

But we're not quite finished. Even at 2,500 or 3,500 hours/year, there's only so much any single superstar individual can take on. And even in the high thin air of very important cases and very important transactions, some are more important—rarer, more consequential, higher-visibility—than others. This is where the multi-million dollar matters go to the stars, the multi-billion matters to the super-stars, and the New York Times front page material to the super-duper stars.

The worlds of professional sports and celebrity entertainment benefit from the empowering reach of mass media distribution in a way law never will, but even in one-on-one personal service industries, as Rosen pointed out, "it is monetarily advantageous to operate in a larger overall market; and it is increasingly advantageous the more talented one is."[33]

> [That's why] the best artists sell their work in the great markets of New York and Paris, not Cincinnati, or the best writers are connected with the primary literary enters such as New York or London. The best doctors, lawyers, and professional athletes should [also] be found more frequently in larger cities.[34]

That was written nearly 40 years ago. Little might Rosen have imagined that the debate over the rewards going to "the 1%" would become a topic of widespread public debate in the second decade of the 21st Century. And theories beyond the superstar phenomenon have been offered to explain the perceived rise in inequality, including arguments that public company CEO's, in bed with compensation consultants who invariably recommend

---

33   *The Economics of Superstars* at 855.
34   Id. at 856.

"above average" pay packages, exert undue influence over complaisant boards; that social norms themselves against higher pay have broken down; or that tax policy is skewed to favor the rich.

It's far afield from my purpose or my desire here to venture into this highly-charged debate, but it might be of some value to sprinkle a bit of data into the discussion—which, I promise, actually bears on superstar lawyer income as well.

We can start by asking whether outsize rewards at the top are skewed by public company CEO compensation, or whether they're occurring to the same degree among privately held enterprises like law firms. (This doesn't actually disprove the theory that CEO's have their boards under their thumb, but it supports the superstar theory if the phenomenon is equally widespread between public and private firms.)

An ingenious analysis of IRS data assumed that income from salary and wages was a fair proxy for public company CEO compensation whereas income from self-employment, partnership, and S corporations stood for private firm management. If you buy that plausible inference, you're better off today at the top of a private firm than a public one. Here's the share of income of the top 0.1% of IRS taxpayers from those two sources at intervals over the past 40 odd years:[35]

	Public	Private
1979	38%	9%
1993	28%	18%
2005	20%	22%

At the very least, this argues against today's 0.1% owing their riches to the directors of public company boards being profligate with shareholder funds—or, more precisely, that was twice as likely 40 years ago as it is now.

---

35   Steven Kaplan and Joshua Rauh, *It's the Market: The Broad-Based Rise in the Return to Top Talent,* Journal of Economic Perspectives, Volume 27, Number 3 (Summer 2013) 35-56 at 39. At the time of publication Kaplan was the Neubauer Family Distinguished Service Professor of Entrepreneurship and Finance at the Unviersity of Chicago Booth School of Business and Rauh was at Professor of Finance at the Stanford Graduate School of Business.

Closer to home, and drawn from privately held enterprises, are these figures showing the average pay of top hedge fund managers and law firm partners over a span of years.[36] The $$ numbers shown first in each column are millions of 2010 dollars and the coefficients in brackets are those amounts relative to average adjusted gross income of the top 0.1%.

	Top 25 hedge fund managers	Average PPP, AmLaw 50 firms
1994		$0.704 [0.268]
1996		$0.784 [0.219]
1998		$0.997 [0.200]
2000		$1.084 [0.167]
2002	$133.7 [34.6x]	$1.099 [0.285]
2004	$289.5 [55.7x]	$1.286 [0.247]
2006	$616.2 [90.3x]	$1.491 [0.218]
2008	$469.8 [82.1x]	$1.449 [0.253]
2010	$882.8 [177.6x]	$1.557 [0.313]
2012	$537.2 [115.7x]	

We aren't doing nearly as well as the hedge fund crowd—in 2010, the top 25 managers earned about four times as much as all the S&P 500 CEOs *combined*—but considering that our income derives from the fruits of labor and not capital, it hasn't been too shabby recently. These figures, of course, largely reflect those at the top of Big Law. Which is the point, isn't it?

Those of you focused on the hedge fund jockeys who are about to rethink this whole JD-degree thing at this point and explore a new career can take heart, however: The lawyer-talent market will never migrate to such extremes as these, for two reasons: First, we're all in the personal service business. What we do cannot be replicated across a wide community of clients at trivial cost, or even a narrow band of clients. It's hands-on, "day labor" (as an irreverent and deeply experienced friend of mine likes to say). Each of us can only be in one place at a time and cannot bill an unlimited number of hours per year. Fixed fee arrangements relax the latter restraint a bit, but the revenue we can receive from a unit of labor is

---

36   Id. at 40, using data from *The American Lawyer* and *Absolute Return + Alpha* magazine.

not as capaciously elastic as it is with celebrities, best-selling authors, and Bill Gross or Steven Cohen.

Second, we don't build our reputations through mass media. Having your firm picked to run the biggest corporate merger of the year or represent the highest-profile litigant will get you press, to be sure, but Lady Gaga and Beyoncé are in the running for the Super Bowl half-time show.

Sorry about that, but perspective is perspective. So let's step back from the most extreme of power-curve distributions and address our world in more familiar terms.

Probably the most widely recognized and commonly used parlance for an unequal distribution with a small number receiving a large amount and a large number receiving a small amount is the "80/20 rule," or the "Pareto principle."

Vilfredo Pareto (1848—1923) was an Italian economist, among other things, who observed that in Italy 20% of the populace owned 80% of the land. It turns out that one could generalize this observation across a wide range of distribution sets, most importantly those of income and wealth. (It also seems to more or less apply to the sizes of cities/towns/villages; the price returns on individual stocks; the size of oil fields; and casualty losses in insurance.)

One of the intriguing properties of 80/20 distributions is that they tend to be "fractal," meaning that no matter what level of resolution—from macro to micro—under which you examine the curve, the function and the pattern remain alike. Put more simply, 80/20 distributions seem to contain more 80/20 distributions within themselves. For our purposes, this means that if partner compensation were to migrate towards such a distribution, not only would the top 20% take home 80% of the income, but the top 20% of the top 20% would take home 80% of that cohort's income, and so on. The data displays basically the same pattern regardless of the scale against which you're plotting it.

This matters because we all know that envy is local and relative, not global and absolute. Rationally, anyone in the top 20% should be grateful at their good fortune and call it a day. But people don't do that; they pay far more attention to how their income stacks up compared to others within their firm or appropriately "adjacent" firms whom they believe are roughly as capable as they are and who apparently perform at a similar level.

Those in the top 20% don't evaluate their compensation vis-à-vis the other 80%, just as the top 1% don't give much thought to the bottom 90%. A host of studies and data support this, but it's hardly necessary since, having all experienced and observed it, we know it's true.[37]

By contrast, when the other person's income is dramatically different—say, 150% or 200% of ours or more—then if we're being honest, we have to admit it's basically understandable and envy doesn't enter the picture.

So what?

So what I think this all adds up to is intense market-driven pressure to pay each partner every dollar right up to the full value of their contribution to the firm. As a friend of mine who, among a host of other admirable qualities, has an economics Ph.D. and is intimately familiar with law firm compensation systems put it in correspondence to me about this topic:

> "The link to compensation is that in competitive markets, a factor [of production] is expected to earn its marginal revenue product."

Phrased with a bit more clarity at the expense of a bit less rigor, a rational profit-maximizing law firm will pay each partner close to if not the entire value to the firm of the revenue that partner brings in. If the firm paid less, the partner could presumably find another conveniently located firm that would accurately recognize and reward his/her full productive value, and if the firm paid more they would find themselves with an almost irresistible incentive to get rid of the (money-losing) partner.

---

37   Numerous studies have shown that when people are asked what level of income would make them satisfied and content, the consensus across almost the entire span—excluding only the truly subsistence-level and "couldn't spend it all in 10 lifetimes" elite—is that a 15% raise would do the trick. Of course, once people experience that 15% raise, their frame of reference rapidly resets and in very short order it calls for *another* 15% to achieve contentment. This shows that yardsticks are comparative and relative, not absolute—and if you bear with me, might tempt you to describe them as "fractal."

A New York hiring partner I know well—who has excelled in that role for decades—expressed the business logic of this in the most succinct possible terms:

> "If you've got the book, we've got the desk."

Now, the real world is not quite so frictionless as this model would require to work precisely as just described. Indeed, I hope the vast majority of you reading this will be grateful that countervailing forces including loyalty to a firm and one's colleagues, reticence and a touch of modesty in the face of the opportunity to extract one's entire "marginal revenue product," and a sincere commitment to nonpecuniary values including client service and professional and intellectual growth and development, will spare us from the further-most unseemly implications of the pure model.

But it's hard to deny the vector trajectory the model points to would have provided a far more accurate description of how Law Land has actually evolved over the past three or four decades, in terms of lateral partner mobility and compensation distributions, than any of the competing rallying cries to law as "a profession and not a business" or expressions of indignation at eroding firm/partner loyalty. In other words, whatever vision of the world your personal values summon forth, the direction of evolution *as we've experienced it* is clear to all, no matter how blinkered your powers of observation.

Implications

The logical implications of this scenario are not abstruse. Among them are:

- Decreasing loyalty of partners to firms, and, in quasi-emotional self-defense or premised on rational calculation, the reciprocal: Decreasing loyalty of firms to partners.

- Increasing awareness by partners of the market value of their skills (and, yes, their "book"), combined with increasing recognition of the bargaining power that bestows on them, and willingness and predisposition to exercise that power in the marketplace.

- Fewer Loyalists among partners, and more Mercenaries.

These forces are far more powerful together than alone. Firms would be irrational to be loyal to partners who are themselves disloyal to the firm, and vice versa. At its extreme, the behavior this dance of the scorpions prescribes isn't fundamentally different from the logic of an arms' race, or the Game Theory 101 warhorse, the prisoners' dilemma. "Better that I take action to protect myself lest you injure me by beating me to it."

In a slightly, but not terribly, different context this logic was expressed by the innovative but very difficult Ferdinand Eberstadt, who began his career as an investment banker at Dillon Read in the 1920's, had his own firm F. Eberstadt & Co. in the 1950's, and was one of those present at the creation of mutual funds as we know them. But he could be tough to deal with:

> "He was constantly chided for not being a good sport in the syndicate game, for driving overly hard bargains, and for going to extraordinary lengths to protect himself when he brought an issue public. His response to these complaints was characteristically caustic: 'I don't want to stick anyone else, and I damn well don't want to get stuck myself.'"[38]

. . .

Is this really the future? For the vast majority of us, it could be. But for a select few, probably not.

Back to *Exodus*, Aaron, and the golden calf.

The super-elite firms who hew to, live out, and are committed heart and head to the Platonic ideal of partnership aren't destined to go down this path. The choice is actually theirs to make: Follow the hard path of the covenant or eat, drink, and revel today.

It's not just aspirational rhetoric and incorporeal values that lead us here; economics provides a basis for this as well.

---

38   Robert Teitelbaum, *Bloodsport: When ruthless dealmakers, shrewd ideologues, and brawling lawyers toppled the corporate establishment* (New York: Public Affairs 2016) at 52, citing Cary Reich, *Financier: the biography of Andre Meyer* (New York: John Wiley & Sons 1983).

Consider the realities, on the ground, of firms seeking to pry partners loose from super-elite firms. Not only are clients of the elite firms institutional clients of the firm and not of any individual, but junior and even senior partners in those firms have never received any training in business development or in cultivating a practice from the ground up. Work has been delivered to them on a silver platter throughout their career. This makes the prospect of their arriving with a rich "book"—or being able to develop one in a financially sane time-frame—unlikely.

Also germane is that with rare exceptions partners in these firms are lifers—they've never really worked anywhere else, and they would face a steep learning curve and potentially an awkward and unproductive transition, to adapt to a different culture and environment.

Put slightly differently and in terms both a bit more precise and sympathetic to the frictions these partners would experience upon being transplanted, they have developed a tremendous stock of what's called "firm-specific capital"—skills, knowledge, and habits of mind that have value only in one particular organization, and nowhere else. It's beside the point that they'd probably never use and perhaps not even recognize this term: If taken from their familiar surroundings, they will be facing a steep and probably unexpected learning curve in the acculturation process.

This is not true, by the way, of most partners in most non-elite firms; the skills they have that clients and the market are willing to pay for tend to be quite portable and transitions to new environments achievable, assuming good intentions and some determined effort all around.

On the compensation dimension, partners in elite firms anticipate benefiting from the lockstep or quasi-lockstep "up escalator" in compensation as well as the generous pension promises these firms have extended—together amounting to an income stream worth tens of millions of dollars which they would forfeit by departing. (The pension benefits are typically conditioned upon compliance with non-compete agreements.)

This leaves us with a talent (labor) market where the large majority of partners have every incentive to (a) maximize their own personal worth in the marketplace, which includes not just (b) the expected present value of the revenue flowing from their book but (c) the proportion of it which is under their control, a/k/a portable.

Firms, meanwhile, will be rational to pay partners right up to or, to the extent transaction and other frictional costs of relocation permit, somewhat less than the full value of the partner's marginal contribution to the firm's income.

We see how this has been playing itself out over the last five or so years as more and more of the Magic Circle and other elite London-based firms have been sidling away from their historic strict lockstep models to allow for mold-breaking compensation packages at the very top, calling them "super points" or using special bonus pools reserved for exceptionally strong performers. Ashurst's announcement that it was going down this road is unusual only for its relative candor:

> Ashurst has voted in changes to its partner remuneration structure, adding an extra 10 points to the top of the equity ladder and introducing a bonus pool.
>
> The changes take the top of the equity ladder from 65 to 75 points for star performers. The bottom of the ladder will remain at 25 points.
>
> The firm has also introduced a bonus pool, which can be used to reward full equity and fixed share partners for strong performances in a particular year. It is understood that the firm will set aside a share of the profit pool to be used for partner bonuses.
>
> A spokesperson for Ashurst said: "This is an evolution of our system, which gives us more flexibility to reward high performance."
>
> The changes are intended to make it easier for the firm to reward strong performers and encourage partner buy-in at a time when average profit per equity partner (PEP) has fallen to its lowest level in more than 10 years.

One partner inside Ashurst said last month: "Given where our PEP currently is, we need something to reward people." He added that the new plateau will be available only "to a very small, exceptional minority".[39]

One presumed member of that "very small, exceptional minority"—albeit at Allen & Overy, not Ashursts—is Scott Zemser, who was at the center of a marquee move of a group of top-of-their-game leveraged finance practitioners in the summer of 2016 from White & Case to A&O to become that firm's new global co-head of leveraged finance. In an interview at the time, he neither celebrated nor bemoaned the arrival of what we might call "the unlocking of lockstep:" He simply recited that that's the way today's world is:

> *There's no question you need to pay what's market.* A&O has shown it's willing to do that and will continue to do that. It's no simple process. My view as a US lawyer competing against the UK firms is that it's not easy to compete against an A&O. They've been there forever and their relationships are deep, but they didn't have this US part. It's just that there's a different remuneration system in the US and it's changed in London the last few years as well. *A&O have proven that they're willing to do what they need to do to continue to build in the US and there's a price for that.*[40]

• • •

Let me add two additional considerations, which are symmetric as between firms and partners, and we'll be in a position to describe and assess what we think of this market.

In our post-Great Financial Reset "New Normal" or "New Neutral" or "New Mediocre" world, clients are in a buyers' market for law firm services. Pricing pressures are intense, the quest for efficiency and value front

---

39   *Ashurst partners agree to extend lockstep and introduce bonus pool for star performers,* LegalWeek (August 2016) (edited for brevity), at http://www.legalweek.com/sites/legalweek/2016/08/02/ashurst-extends-lockstep-and-introduces-bonus-pool/

40   *Legal Business,* "Allen & Overy's Scott Zemser talks leveraged finance, lockstep and competing in the US," August 2016 (emphasis supplied), http://www.legalbusiness.co.uk/index.php/lb-blog-view/7293-q-a-a-o-s-scott-zemser-talks-leveraged-finance-lockstep-and-competing-in-the-us

of mind, and tolerance for slack and firms' ascending a learning curve on the client's dime nonexistent. In a nutshell, clients are increasingly sophisticated and discriminating among law firms and they want to hire *the* firm with deep and genuine expertise in the particular array of practice specialties their matter requires. General practice, full-service, one-size-fits-all firms who are a destination for nothing in particular find their value difficult to articulate to clients.[41]

The impetus towards symmetrical firm/partner behavior in such an environment is self-evident: Specialization and depth win over generalists and (shallow) breadth. Simply put, lawyers have every motivation to develop a reputation for being among the "go-to" experts in XYZ area, while firms have the complementary motivation to fashion themselves into, ideally, the "category killer" or "integrated focus" models.

Now we can finally ask: So what does such a market look like?

We're all free agents now

Actually we have a high-profile talent market which might provide some clues: That between Major League Baseball teams and players. Consider the parallels:

- The supply of talent is limited by several factors:
    o A relatively small minority of the population has both the inclination and the threshold ability to even consider the career;
    o An extended period of single-minded professional training is required before individuals can enter the market;
    o Beyond that, it takes an additional span of years before the quality of an individual's performance can be reliably assessed.

- The number of "major league" teams/firms is limited by constraints on how many the fans/clients can support economically. (I put aside the notorious MLB antitrust exemption, which dates back nearly a century, to *Federal Baseball Club v. National League*, 259 U.S. 200 (1922); the current cap on the number of MLB teams is 30, set in 1998.)

41　　This paragraph is a succinct summary of the arguments advanced in my two prior books, *Growth Is Dead: Now What?* (New York, Adam Smith, Esq., LLC 2013) and *A New Taxonomy: The Seven Law Firm Business Models* (New York, Adam Smith, Esq., LLC 2014).

- Some teams/firms are more prestigious than others.

- Some teams/firms can afford to pay more than others.

I won't press the analogy beyond what it will bear, because of necessity it must remain primarily a thought experiment and not an empirical inquiry. Data on the distribution of MLB *player* salaries—as opposed to total team payrolls, which is widely publicized—is very difficult to assemble, and data on the distribution of *individual* AmLaw 200 partners' compensation is nonexistent and probably destined to remain an eternal mystery.

But if we follow the train of thought for at least a few more mental cycles, one intriguing parallel would be that of how individual talent multiplies value. MLB superstars have mass media exposure on their side, something AmLaw superstars don't, at least yet, although some I've met couldn't see that day come soon enough. On the other hand, marquee partners generate many many multiples of their own billable time for the firm, and not even a .400 hitter gets his team-mates a single additional at-bat.

A more important dimension of the analogy focuses on team vs. individual performance. Here the logic of talent markets suggests the AmLaw superstar deserves a distribution of compensation even more highly skewed to their advantage than our MLB superstars.

Baseball, classically, is a team sport; only pitchers are consistently recognized as making uniquely individual contributions, and even their ability to determine wins and losses is notoriously tangential.

Law Land? In the Platonic ideal partnerships, a team sport.

In the other 90+% of partnerships? Superstars are the coin of the realm: Think golf or tennis more than baseball or football. We still recognize the names of legendary advocates or advisors, but many of us would be hard-pressed to identify with confidence the firms where they worked.

Let's move this discussion from the economic dynamics of this talent market to how it feels and works for individuals and firms living in the market every day. The salient characteristics of this type of market—in terms of how participants experience it—include some most people would find unattractive:

- Very little or no institutional loyalty.

- Incentives tilted strongly towards maximizing one's value as a solo actor at the expense of investing in firm-specific capital.

- A strong albeit rebuttable presumption in favor of the "highest bidder" landing the talent.

- Lock-in of the latently perilous centrifugal force effects of no institutional loyalty, which becomes an essentially permanent condition of existence for most law firms.

But some positive attributes as well:

- Quite possibly, rational firms and individuals will use the very liquid talent market to sort themselves out by focusing on the types of "position players" they need: Firms/teams who need a shortstop, a closing pitcher, a private equity guru, or a fund formation specialist will pay more for individuals with those skills than firms/teams with generalized or non-specific "talent upgrade" desires. This would be a good thing. Ideally, we should all root for assets to migrate to their highest and best uses.

- Talent being able to extract its marginal revenue product—as it should in a competitive market, and something to be celebrated if you're "talent" and not "firm."

The highly liquid, transparent, and active lateral partner is here to stay. Every year seems to record a new high in lateral partner moves in the AmLaw 200 (2015, the latest data available, was true to form) and with 96% of AmLaw 200 firms identifying lateral partner recruitment as either very or moderately important to their revenue growth strategies, don't look for a change any time soon.[42] And this despite the remarkable disconnect that only 28% of managing partners believe lateral hiring has been effective at their firms. This brings to mind the title of Jimmy Breslin's book

---

42   "Lateral Warfare," ALM Legal Intelligence (July 2016), at http://www.law.com/law/sites/ali/2016/07/21/lateral-warfare/

chronicling the 1962 New York Mets impressively inept first season, *Can't Anybody Here Play This Game?* What on earth is going on?

Perhaps the most exhaustive empirical study of lateral movement ever performed in the industry, looking at more than 30,000 individual moves over 12 years, was led by Prof. William Henderson of Indiana/Maurer School of Law, and summarized in the February 2015 *American Lawyer*.[43] The highlights:

- "We have uncovered zero statistical evidence that an aggressive lateral partner hiring strategy in and of itself is associated with greater law firm profitability. If the goal is higher profits relative to peer firms, or even higher revenue per lawyer, a lateral partner hiring strategy based on volume is not working."

- "That said, [it] is significantly correlated with one market outcome: higher gross revenues. This is a very important piece of clinical information. We think law firm managers engage in lateral partner hiring (or acquiesce to the lateral partner hiring urged by powerful partners) because they feel they have to. Such partners came of age during a period of rapid industry growth. Growth feels good. Yet for several years it has been largely absent in most firms."

- "[On the other hand,] when it's coupled with an effective vetting and integration process, it can increase profitability. Problem is, the typical vetting or integration process is not effective. If it were, higher lateral volume would lead to better firm-level results."

We seem addicted to a costly and disruptive behavior pattern that nearly three-quarters of managing partners believe is a failure at their firms, yet we evidently can't bring ourselves to instill the discipline of an "effective vetting and integration process." Is it that there simply *is* no way to consistently and reliably evaluate talent in advance?

Actually, the venture capital and private equity industries have come up with an empirically based approach. When they're assessing potential investments, quality of management talent at target companies is the most reliable predictor of investment outcome. So the investment firms face

---

43   William Henderson & Chris Zorn, *A Prescription for Laterals,* The American Lawyer (February 2015).

ongoing, repeated, and systemic challenges in evaluating managerial talent. How do they proceed?

In the mid-1990's one Geoff Smart was earning a Ph.D. in psychology and for his dissertation topic chose to model the financial returns of VC firms as a function of the type of human capital due diligence they performed in advance of investing. The most widespread approach was what he labeled the "art critic" model: Gut feeling and intuition. This produced mediocre, almost random, returns.

The strongest returns, in contrast, went to VCs employing the "airline captain" model: Lengthy, methodical, relatively invariant, non-discretionary and objective checklists. "Airline captains" outperformed "art critics" by a factor of three, and the company Smart founded out of his research counts Blackstone, Bain Capital, KKR, Goldman Sachs, and Citadel among its clients.

We may seem to have wandered afield from Law Land, but I think not.

Most firms by far are still art critics when it comes to hiring, but a few have at least dabbled at approaching talent recruitment like an airline captain. If they stick to it, they will be the ones who more consistently find the position players they need and who waste less time and fewer resources seeking out and paying top dollar for fungible B players. VC's were forced to move to the airline captain model by competition: Your performance can't consistently lag your peer group if you hope to attract investors for your next fund.

One can hope a similar dynamic might take hold in Law Land, and that a greater hit rate in finding just those lawyers optimally suited to each firm's platform might become apparent through competitive outperformance. At that point other firms might find the courage to stand up to the internal lobby nostalgic for the art critic mindset and adopt techniques to produce lasting matches of the right firm with the right talent. I said "one can hope" for a reason: Isn't that what we all want out of our careers?

But we're not quite done with the issue of talent.

First, beware the elementary mistake of overpaying for A players. I opened this chapter indirectly alerting you to beware the Atlantic Records/Yankees effect. Even talent of the caliber of A-Rod and the Stones can be a curse at the wrong price.

If only discipline were our middle name.

Second, I talked earlier about asymmetry in the bargain commonly struck between most partners and most firms: It's deeply one-sided, all in favor of the partners all the time. But how might the logic of the talent market change that?

Consider the tiresome riddle posed by people thinking they're cute, "Do you hire the lawyer or the law firm?" The answer of course is "both." (Going back to our sports analogies: Is it the New England Patriots or Tom Brady that produces so many winning seasons? Stupid question; it's both.)

Clients hire lawyers they can repose confidence in at firms with pedigrees sufficient to match the caliber of the stakes at issue in the client's matter. As clients become more discerning and discriminating, the following market dynamic kicks in. I quote again from Brad Karp's keynote at the Bloomberg *Big Law* Summit held in New York in June 2016:

> We have seen the exodus of key partners from elite law firms and an unprecedented shuffling of clients between the haves and the have-nots. The gap between the elite firms and the next tier is widening every year.

In other words, A-team lawyers are finding they need to be part of an A-team firm, and A-team firms realize their calling card is A-team partners. Brad minced no words about this:

> We focus continually on talent; talent has been an indispensable ingredient to our firm's success. Ours is a talent business.

We may find ourselves inescapably drawn into a world where it was never a better time to be a superstar and never a more mediocre time to be on the B team. Evidence? The widening gap between the elite and the next tier.

The elite firms gravitate towards, and pin their success on, the Platonic ideal partnership model. The next tier, and all the other tiers, not so much.

Start by imagining if managing partners at non-elite, non-Platonic ideal firms, the large majority by far, assessed their firm's rank in the pecking order with cold-blooded realism, and not through delusional aspirational lenses. Maybe this would begin to tilt the partner/firm asymmetry back a bit in favor of the firms. How so? They would realize/ admit they're not in the market for superstars, they're in the market for B team players. And set partner expectations about compensation, and performance standards, accordingly.

If your instincts are to recoil—this would be harsh, uncharitable, disdainful of everyone who's not a superstar—let me elaborate in hopes you'll adjust your perspective.

For starters, may we adopt the perspective of clear-eyed realism of that hypothetical managing partner at a next tier firm and acknowledge that just as the firm they're managing is not elite, not every lawyer is going to be a superstar? Talent is unequally distributed and unequally cultivated, and time and chance happeneth to them all.

The Cornell economics professor Robert Frank (along with many others including economics and public policy professor Philip Cook of Duke) have published entire books and devoted a decade or more to analyzing and elaborating upon the implications of this age-old fact of human life, and how the consequences are now being compounded by two relatively new factors, first that technology has amplified small differences in performance and second that there's heightened competition for the services of the top performers.[44]

> The same pattern of income growth [inequality] we've seen for the population as a whole has been replicated for virtually every subgroup that's been studied. It holds for dentists, real-estate agents, authors, attorneys, newspaper columnists, musicians,

---

44   Robert Frank & Philip Cook, *The Winner-Take-All Society: Why the Few at the Top Get So Much More Than the Rest of Us,* New York, Penguin: 1996, and Frank, *The Darwin Economy: Liberty, Competition, and the Common Good,* Princeton, Princeton University Press: 2011.

and plastic surgeons. It holds for electrical engineers and English majors.

Welcome to the "Barbell" World?

One of the more memorable and notorious comments coming out of the celebrated Dewey collapse was Jeffrey Kessler's unapologetic defense of the extreme pay spread between the highest and the lowest paid partners at Dewey, which reached a ratio of 25:1 and beyond.

Kessler (Columbia B.A./J.D.) was a partner at Weil Gotshal before moving to Dewey Ballantine in 2003; following the 2007 LeBoeuf merger he become chair of the combined firm's global litigation department and one of the "Gang of Four" that constituted Dewey's office of the chairman.

One of the most prominent sports lawyers in the country, he defended the firm's "barbell" compensation distribution in an interview with *The New York Times,* saying there was "immense pressure" to reward the big rainmakers who cultivated clients while partners who "did the fundamental work" "were worth less and less." He noted that A-Rod was paid far more compared to his teammates than Mickey Mantle had been in the 1950s:

> "The value for the stars has gone up, while the value of service partners has gone down."[45]

Whatever else you think about Mr. Kessler's philosophy—and many hastened to point out that his stated views just happened to align squarely with his self-interest—he's right about the trend of compensation in major league sports, and in BigLaw.

He's also talking about *non* Platonic ideal partnerships. The late Francis X. H. Musselman (1925—2013), chairman of Milbank from 1970—1984, also served as trustee in bankruptcy of the estate of Finley Kumble, one of the early shooting star flameout firms (discussed earlier), which at its end had a high:low partner pay ratio of 13:1. Fran said "whatever else you call that, it's *not* a partnership." Indeed.

---

45   *Dealbook,* May 9, 2012: http://dealbook.nytimes.com/2012/05/09/deweys-jeffrey-kessler-heading-to-winston-strawn/

But let's follow Mr. Kessler's logic out.

What does this mean for the individual, particularly those who find out they're not superstars? This realization may come in several forms: One can recognize it quite early on (clarity and self-awareness from the start) or discover it only after a time (striving admirably until the results become inarguable) or surrender late in the game to the inevitable. My own belief is that how one reacts to these paths in life is within one's control, and is a decision not a submission. One can choose resignation and adopt the mantle of the defeated or choose to put your best foot forward and excel at making the most valuable contribution you can.

Second, the literature on how much of career satisfaction depends on factors having nothing to do with compensation is persuasive and growing. Compensation needs to be "sufficient"—adequate and fair by market standards. But beyond that people rank it consistently near the bottom of their top ten sources of career satisfaction. What counts are intangibles such as having a sense of autonomy, achieving mastery over a discipline, the respect of one's colleagues and peers. We all know this to be true in our hearts; we could actually pay heed.

Finally, do we really want to measure our self-worth by this year's take-home pay? Isn't there somewhat more to life than that?

I leave the last word on the consequences of the talent market to: Who else?

> The great mob of mankind are the admirers and worshippers...of wealth and greatness [paying lip-service to wisdom and virtue].
>
> There is scarce any man who does not respect more the rich and the great, than the poor and the humble. With most men the presumption and vanity of the former are much more admired, than the real and solid merit of the latter. It is scarce agreeable to good morals or even good language...that mere wealth and greatness, abstracted from merit and virtue, deserve our respect.
>
> —Adam Smith[46]

---

46   *Theory of Moral Sentiments* at I:79 (London: 1759).

"The greatest improvement in the productive powers of labour, and the greater part of the skill, dexterity, and judgment with which it is anywhere directed, or applied, seem to have been the effects of the divi-sion of labour ... To take an example, therefore, from a very trifling manufacture; but one in which the division of labour has been very often taken notice of the trade of the pin-maker; a workman not educated to this business, nor acquainted with the use of the machinery employed in it, could scarce, perhaps, with his utmost industry, make one pin in a day, and certainly could not make twenty. But in the way in which this business is now carried on, ... one man draws out the wire, another straights its, a third cuts it, a fourth points it, [etc., with the re-sult that] I have seen a small manufactory of this kind where ten men only were employed [and] though they were very poor, and therefore but indifferently accommodated with the necessary machinery, they could, when they exerted themselves, make among them about twelve points of pins in a day, [or] upwards of forty-eight thousand pins."

—Adam Smith, An Inquiry into the Nature and Causes of the Wealth of Nations, (London: 1776; The Modern Library: New York 1994), Book I, Chapter 1.

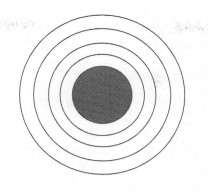

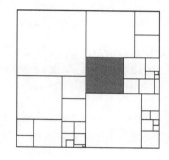

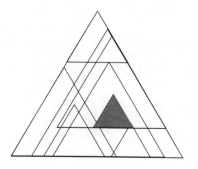

Differentiation and Speciation Win

Among the charming economic eccentricities Law Land splendidly exhibits is how we all seem to imagine we follow a single, quite undifferentiated, business model. This is a bit of a caricature but we'll use it as a departure point because it too often is painfully close to the truth:

- Hire the best lawyers you can find, or else the best you can afford;

- Go after the highest value client work you can find, or else the highest that clients will trust you with;

- Bill by the hour, a cost-plus model with profit built right in (provided only that collections don't go into freefall) because other ways of pricing are complicated and unpredictable and have no track record of comfort and familiarity;

- Raise your rates every year because your lawyers are presumably getting more experienced plus we don't know how else to grow revenue;

- Disdain the contribution and input of "non-lawyers" on the business side of your firm because lawyers know best about anything and everything; and

- Dismiss proposals for new ways of working, even slight adjustments, until they've already been widely adopted elsewhere.

Exaggeration?

I plead guilty, with an explanation.

My last book, *A New Taxonomy: The seven law firm business models* (New York: Adam Smith, Esq., 2014), was structured around the premise that there actually is more than one law firm business model, and this chapter of this book is meant to expand on that idea.

Taxonomy introduced the following general types of firms:

- Global players
    - Spanning three or more continents
    - Great heft and deep capabilities across economically important sectors
    - Widespread brand name recognition

- Capital markets firms
    - Headquartered in a global financial center
    - Practice heavily focused on banking, finance, and securities
    - Often tied historically or otherwise to an investment bank

- Kings of their hill
    - Headquartered in cities that are national but not global, destinations
    - Catering to upper/upper-middle market corporations and high net worth families
    - Solidly embedded in their local markets

- Boutiques
    - Firms that do one and really only one thing exceptionally well
    - Size not a criterion
    - A 1,000-lawyer "boutique?" Sure
    - Overwhelming agreement on what "they one thing" they do is

- Category killers
    - Targeting one broad practice
    - Hungry and effective acquirers
    - Ultimately persuading other firms to abandon the field to them
    - And the model *works*

- The hollow middle
    - Generic, "full service," one-size-fits-all
    - Not a destination for anything in particular
    - Don't benefit from "flight to quality" *or* from "flight to economy"

- Integrated focus
    - Designed around an external orientation—an industry or an intuitively distinctive practice area
    - Focused on—and only on—the practice areas that their chosen industry requires
    - Creating a clear brand; clients "get it"

In the *Taxonomy* book itself, I also specified the following rules for using the categories and thinking about where one's own firm is and where it might be desirable for it to migrate towards.

The overall rules are only three:

1. No category guarantees success and no category is a sentence to failure; we have successful and struggling examples of firms fitting all seven models.
2. Any given firm can have a leg planted in more than one category, although probably not in more than two. This gives us the final rule:
3. Firms can, over time and with concerted effort, migrate from one category to another, although the barriers to entry vary greatly across categories.

To rehearse a bit more what should be the top-of-mind issues for people running these firms:

- Global players
    - How many of such firms does the world actually need? (Apparently fewer than many thought a decade ago.)
    - On the plus side, sheer scale is a barrier to entry for newcomers.
    - But daunting managerial complexity is and will remain an ever-present reality (Brexit, anyone?).

- Capital markets
    - Has the door closed? If you're not already in the tent, barriers to entry include
        - Deep and enduring ties to at least one important financial institution with global operations
        - Intimate local/cultural/socioeconomic "fit" within the capital markets culture of the key home city
        - Building an impressive store of reputational capital

- Kings of their hill
    - What if the home-grown client base migrates out from under the firm?
        - This is outside anyone's control (including in important ways the clients themselves)
            - » Cf. upstate New York and the Midwest rust belt to the Sun Belt
    - Can be a big fish, but will always be in a smaller pond
    - Risk of slow talent drain as the most ambitious and capable relocate to more cosmopolitan, sophisticated economic centers

- Boutiques
  - Will there be a second generation?
    - Need to avoid the cult of personality around founders
  - Focus
    - Must relentlessly say no to anything other than "the one thing," no matter how passionately partners or clients plead
  - Succession planning is imperative, not just good management hygiene

- Category killers
  - Must resist temptations to dilute highly specialized focus
  - Can afford to make serious investments in process optimization and efficiency in the chosen practice area
  - Natural magnets for talent in their chosen niche—lawyers who might have been peripheral elsewhere can be core in firms like this

- The hollow middle
  - The "hollow middle" appellation identifies a different type of creature than the other six taxonomical categories, which runs the risk of creating (understandable) conceptual confusion. The other six describe the firms themselves in each category—Davis Polk is a Capital Markets firm, White & Case a Global Player, and so on.
    - The phrase hollow middle, by contrast, describes an industry structure: Strictly speaking, there is no such thing as a "hollow middle" *firm*. There are only firms occupying a position in the industry's ecosystem that will become untenable if the industry migrates fully to a hollow middle structure.
  - So what exactly does a hollow middle industry looks like? It describes a marketplace where customers segment themselves into a group which strongly prefers high end products or

services and another group which only requires satisfactory features—but expects them to be priced accordingly.[47]

- o Another way of describing this dynamic is that a "polarized equilibrium" spontaneously comes into existence, between a clear set of high quality, high price providers and another equally clear set of "good enough" quality, high-value providers—with not much in the middle. Audi, BMW, Lexus, and Porsche do nicely, and so do Hyundai and Kia; it turns out no one really needs Oldsmobile, Plymouth, or Pontiac.
- o Not only is this a highly common structure across the economy, but it turns out to be a highly durable structure once it kicks in
  - Tough to establish a blue chip pedigree from a standing start
  - And it's tough to challenge high-value mass providers without launching on a daunting scale almost from the start.

- · Integrated focus
  - o Requires great discipline
    - "Strategy means saying no"
  - o Have to choose your industry focus wisely
    - With a view towards the long term
  - o High intrinsic profitability but disturbing the spoils can be challenging.

· · ·

There's the 30,000-foot version. Let's explore in more detail what intrinsic challenges and opportunities tend to come with pursuing each of the seven models.

As for **global players**, by and large since the Great Financial Reset of 2008-2009, they've retrenched. The Magic Circle have, as a whole, closed as many existing offices as they've opened new. Ranks of equity partners have

---

47   A detail which has no effect on the industry's structure but which clarifies which customers veer high-end and which migrate towards satisfactory: *It depends* on the context and purpose the customer has in mind. The very same customer could quite logically and rationally have a non-negotiable preference for Tiffany or Cartier when buying a diamond engagement ring, but buy all their other jewelry at Zales or Costco. This also describes corporations hiring law firms—which is indeed the whole point of this section: Sometimes only a Cravath-class pedigree will do, but most of the time price matters and good enough will be good enough.

been trimmed in historically unprecedented ways (this is hardly unique to global players, but it wasn't supposed to happen to them).

Most telling is that no firm I know of that's not already a global player aspires to be one. Ten years ago that statement would have been preposterous; the aspirants were legion.

Why the change? Enter reality. Managing globe-spanning networks of 20, 30, or more offices is more complex, demanding, frangible, and just plain exhausting than we knew. (I once asked the managing partner of one of these firms where he considered his "home" office to be, and he replied, "American Airlines.")

Being a global player also means being, well, "global," and that brings with it some of the implications one could predict from the behavior of diversified portfolios—which is essentially what these firms have constructed, in the form of their worldwide office footprints. A widely diversified portfolio means having offices in heavy-duty capital markets centers including New York, London, and Hong Kong, which produce high fees and (unless rudely mismanaged) high profits.

But that same firm will also be in many if not all of: A cross-section of domestic US offices, perhaps a few non-London UK offices, mainland China, Australia, the Mideast, Africa, and the EU (which remains a mixture of historically, linguistically, and socioeconomically disparate states with no known solvent that might bring them closer together). Almost never will the economies of all those regions be rising or falling in lockstep, so the result is performance that's neither spectacular nor dreadful, but likely somewhere in between.

We can see this graphically in a 10-year chart of the profits per partner of the Magic Circle vs. the US elite, who tend to have far more focused footprints:[48]

48   Chart of the author's creation: Data adapted from *Legal Business (UK)*, "Global 100: Hitting the wall" July 2016, at http://www.legalbusiness.co.uk/index.php/analysis/6919-hitting-the-wall

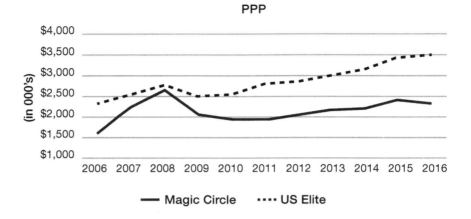

One particular dimension of having a global footprint is the stress on your reported financial results inflicted by the careless volatility of the foreign exchange markets. Inevitably, some region's currency is up as another's is down; partners on the short end of the stick don't see why they should personally suffer financially at the whim of impersonal markets, and partners on the winning end (that year) are equally quick to point out the favorable jump in reported results from their offices. It becomes difficult and tiresome to argue that it all washes out over time.

Shortly before publication, we saw a particularly dramatic example of currency volatility: Just as the Magic Circle firms seemed to be finally making incremental headway in building their New York offices, Brexit. The British pound went from $1.49 the day before the vote to $1.32 in 72 hours (a 13% drop).

Capital markets firms face their own challenges. Yes, it can be a wonderful business driver for a law firm to be joined at the hip to a major investment bank, but financial services is one of the most volatile businesses this side of oil and gas.

Goldman Sachs and Sullivan & Cromwell's relationship goes back to the 1906 Sears Roebuck IPO and before, and was rock-solid throughout the 20th Century and into the 21st. Their offices in lower Manhattan are barely a block apart and Wall Street lore has it that some S&C partners had internal Goldman phone lines on their desks. Secondments of S&C associates to Goldman's legal department were virtually a continuous practice—until 2008, when it reportedly stopped dead, and didn't revive for a few years.

Similarly, Milbank's relationship with Chase Manhattan Bank (and by extension the Rockefeller family) was so close that for decades Milbank's offices were in One Chase Manhattan Plaza at Nassau and Liberty Streets; Milbank lawyers didn't even have to go outside to visit the client.

Then of course there's Freshfields' relationship with the Bank of England, going back to 1742, a year when the entire population of Manhattan Island was about 11,000 souls (putting "Old World" and "New World" in some perspective).

Then there are the capital markets "wannabe" firms, who typically look at the London's and New York's of the world from a distance and see only billing rates over $1,000/hour and marquee clients and deals. They don't see the pressure-cooker competition for talent and for those same name-brand clients, nor the fabled 40% "Manhattan tax" (it's a safe operating assumption that everything—everything—costs 40% more in Manhattan) nor—and this may be their most glaring blind spot of all—the ineffable and indispensable prerequisite that a firm be in the elite inner circle before it can play in the elite inner circle.

Kings of their hill, the firms catering to sophisticated upper and upper-middle market corporations and to very high net-worth individuals and families—but headquartered in non-global cities—by and large enjoyed a spectacular run for many decades from the beginning of the 20th Century onward. Understandably: They have a lot going for them as a law firm business model. If they rarely work on deals or litigations with national visibility, they're still one of the biggest fish in their pond. That means, among other things, that they're suffused with intimate knowledge of their local market and enjoy deeply embedded personal relationships in the city and community, with their partners traveling in circles ranging from politicians to leading business executives.

Less visible but, I believe, far more consequential in terms of gluing clients to these firms are networks of firm/client contacts shared in non-commercial, apolitical social and community venues ranging from children's sports leagues to churches and synagogues to country clubs and sometimes "preferred" vacation/second home locales. Literally, they live with their clients; how can an outside firm trump that?

The short answer is outside firms rarely can, unless they care to invest years cultivating local presence, but the longer answer is that very often they don't have to and wouldn't want to. Fortunately for our economy and standard of living, but unfortunately for many kings of their hill, cities and metropolitan areas are dynamic: Pick almost any top-50 (per the US Census) urban area and the odds are high it's risen or fallen by sometimes a substantial amount over any period measured in decades.

"Decades" may strike you as an excessively prolonged timeframe, but careers are measured in decades and we can all hope that solid client relationships can last as long as well. Now, if you're a king of your hill that years ago planted your flag in a metropolitan area that has exploded, may I commend you on your foresight and perspicacity (Silicon Valley when it was "Apricot Valley," anyone?). On the other hand, for those of you on the short end of the Walmart/globalization of manufacturing/ Sun Belt hollowing out the Rust Belt phenomenon, what on earth *were* you thinking?

Seriously, metropolitan areas' fortunes can rise and fall dramatically. Here's proof:[49]

Top 10 US Cities 2014				
Rank	City	2014 Pop. (est.)	1950 Pop.	Rank in 1950
1	New York	8,491,079	7,891,957	1
2	Los Angeles	3,928,864	1,970,358	4
3	Chicago	2,722,389	3,620,962	3
4	Houston	2,239,558	596,163	14
5	Philadelphia	1,560,297	2,071,605	3
6	Phoenix	1,537,058	106,818	99
7	San Antonio	1,436,697	408,442	25

49   All of this data comes from the US Census Bureau (census.gov) in one form or another, although much was selected and reformatted by the author. *See, e.g. Population for the 100 Largest Cities and Other Urban Places in the United States: 1790 to 1990,* at https://www.census.gov/population/www/documentation/twps0027/ twps0027.html.

Top 10 US Cities 2014				
8	San Diego	1,381,069	334,387	31
9	Dallas	1,281,047	434,46222	22
10	San Jose	1,015,785	n/a	(not in top 100)

Or, we can look at the data conversely, as it were. Here are some selected cities' rankings in 1950 and in 2015:

City	1950	2015
Detroit	5	18
Cleveland	7	48
St. Louis	8	>50
Pittsburgh	12	>50
Buffalo	13	>50
Cincinnati	18	>50
Denver	24	21
Rochester	32	>50
Atlanta	33	39

The point of course is that no one can foretell the fortunes of a metropolitan area years down the road, any more than one can predict with assurance the client demand for a practice specialty or area of substantive expertise.

Boutiques, in the sense I use the term, have several common characteristics:

- They do one and essentially only one thing, but
  - They do it exceptionally well, and
  - Everyone knows what that "one thing" is.

- They can be large or small, high end or low end.

- At least in the first generation, charismatic leadership is almost a prerequisite.

- Aside from the charisma-quotient hurdle, barriers to entry in formation of a boutique are exceedingly low: For all practical purposes, nonexistent.

- But/and because of the charisma issue, the common and number one challenge embedded in their business model is succession planning and specifically surviving the transition to the second generation of leadership.

- Sticking to that "one thing" is intrinsically linked to a specific benefit and a specific risk:
  - o Clarity of focus makes it relatively trivial to communicate the firm's brand essence;
  - o But that focus must be enforced rigorously against dilution, and with no meaningful diversification of practice expertise, cyclical downturns can be harsh indeed.

Aside from these distinguishing features, one is actually left with very little original or insightful to say about boutiques that has not already been described elsewhere, usually by authors of great erudition far more immersed in this particular topic than I.

All I will add by way of macro perspective is, first, that the "boutique" business model is almost ubiquitous throughout the economy, from enormous industry sectors to the smallest, and by and large they seem able to peacefully coexist with the largest players.

Consider Walmart and Costco alongside Cartier, Tiffany, and your local farmers' market; Toyota, Ford and GM vs. Ferrari, Aston Martin, and perhaps—the jury will probably be out for some years—Tesla; Starbucks with Stumptown, Intelligentsia, or Blue Bottle roasters; Simon & Schuster, HarperCollins, and Penguin Random House next to Spark Press, BlueBullsEye, Pen Name, and Cactus Rain; Marriott/Starwood, InterContinental, Hilton, and Wyndham vs. Andaz, Morgans, and pure one-offs such as (in New York) the Library, NoMad, Giraffe, Refinery, Crosby Street, Elysee, Mark, OutNYC, and on and on.

Second, the wall between mega- and boutique is actually punctuated with revolving doors. Boutiques hive off from the Magic Circle or the AmLaw 200 and other boutiques are acquired and absorbed right back in. Particularly in Corporate Land, where innovation receives a more self-conscious premium, boutiques occasionally serve as sources of innovation through imitation or acquisition—the proven strategy of "if you can't beat 'em, buy 'em."

You might think of this as the obverse of no material barriers to entry for boutiques; maintaining the optionality of being acquired means no material barriers to exit.

Category killers, a term borrowed from the retailing industry, refers to firms providing soup-to-nuts service in one and only one particular practice area: Home Depot and Lowe's, Staples and Office Depot/OfficeMax, Petco and Petsmart, Toys "R" Us, Bed Bath and Beyond, and on and on. Why does there seem to be a killer for almost every category? (Window blinds? Check. Wood flooring? Check.)

Because the concept works. Customers get it, and more important, customers have shown they like it. It's easy to understand why, but in retailing and in Law Land.

First, category killers promise one-stop shopping *for what they offer.* A misapprehension was abroad for many years, decades really, that one-stop shopping was the desideratum for almost any grouping of products or services that could be shoehorned into a single box. (Remember "financial supermarkets?") In Law Land, the analog was the prevalent belief around the turn of the 21st Century that globe-spanning full service firms would own the future, as clients wouldn't want to have to pick and choose among the myriad of options for local counsel or practice area gurus. Small, provincial, narrowly focused firms had no significant future on the stage of law's main events.

It turned out clients were more discriminating (more sophisticated, if you will) and quite willing to take some trouble to pick best of breed among various position players when the stakes justified it. Category killers can remain viable and indeed strong where they choose to play provided they have the discipline to invest in being able to deliver consistent, deep, and broad expertise in their chosen field. This means:

- Building and sustaining impressive depth in their field.

- Undercutting rivals to deliver value, not through the blunt instrument of discounting but through the much more powerful and competitively deadly process of investing in process management.
  o Utilizing their focus on one expertise to target those investments;
  o Keeping it up with "continuous improvement;" and
  o Pushing work to the lowest possible level while at the same time improving quality.

"One-stop shopping" harbored a grain of truth: Yes, clients readily understand and are delighted to patronize firm that does that one thing they need at the moment exceptionally well because it's that law firm's core competence and not a peripheral, ancillary, or opportunistic offering. But by no means confuse this with a preference for "shopping" for *everything* under one roof.

Second, category killers can—and this is presumably the end game for the best of them—create their own barriers to entry for would-be competitors by becoming such an obvious and compelling choice for (say) employment issues, tech startups in Silicon Valley, or private equity fund formation, that there's very little oxygen left in the market for rivals whose expertise is more diffuse. Clients' reasoning is captured by the catch phrase, "why go anywhere else?"

Third, a somewhat subtler but equally powerful dynamic can set in helping raise the walls and deepen the moats surrounding a category killer: Gradual migration of talent. This belatedly dawned on me a few years ago when I was attending the annual partner retreat of one such firm. As I circulated among the attendees over the weekend, I often asked by way of opening a conversation "how long have you been here?" and the predictable corollary, "where did you come from?"

Turns out, little did I suspect, this was more than a foray inviting small talk. With surprising prevalence, the partners who weren't home-grown had moved from firms that halfway knowledgeable industry observers would deem more prestigious, higher-profile, broader in practice area expertise and capability, and, in the headhunters' poxed word, all-around better "platforms." So what gives?

What gives is simple on a moment's reflection: Those firms were *not* better platforms for these practitioners specializing in the killer category practice area: At the higher-profile firms, they were peripheral: Here, they were core. The partners at that retreat knew exactly what they were doing when they relocated: They were finding their highest and best use. Adam Smith would approve. And the more elite firms would be sucked dry of talent in that category.

Finally, people often wonder how category killers and boutiques intersect. Very directly.

Category killers are a subset of boutiques, but worth segregating out as a distinct variety of business model (so I believe) because they stand for and communicate a different positioning in the marketplace than boutiques. "Boutiques" embrace both small firms designed as the legal equivalent of special-purpose SWAT teams, as well as much larger and more capacious firms identified with marquee founders. Thus:

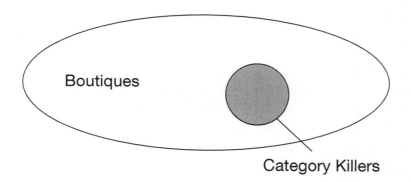

And now we come inevitably, to the **Hollow Middle.** When I polled my online readers a few years ago on the occasion of the impending publication of *Taxonomy* and asked them to nominate firms by name for each of the seven categories, Hollow Middle received both the most guarded and the most amusing responses, including "The AmLaw 40 and above," "firms Harvard 1L's haven't heard of," and "the rest of us." It would be dealing in kryptonite to name names here, so I won't—and remember, firms can always evolve from one category to another—but I will describe the characteristics of these firms and try to supply a larger macroeconomic framework around this concept.

For starters, Hollow Middle is the answer to the classic form of SAT question, "which item in this grouping doesn't belong with the rest?" That's because the other six categories are names for and descriptors of the kinds of firms falling under each umbrella, whereas Hollow Middle describes not a type of firm but an *industry structure*. In that sense, it's technically incorrect and a somewhat tortured use of language to label XYZ a "hollow middle firm." But it's convenient shorthand, people will do it, everyone understands what they mean, and so we won't be persnickety.

What did I mean a moment ago by "industry structure?" In economics and in strategic business analysis, an industry's structure describes how the players in it relate to one another. The two polar opposites are monopoly and perfect competition, which are highly stylized and somewhat artificial constructs, rarely found in the wild, but still instructive as models to get the mental gears engaged. Vastly more common in developed economies are varieties of oligopoly (a few suppliers, essentially undifferentiated products) and the oxymoronically described "monopolistic competition" (many suppliers, products differentiated slightly and mostly through branding, hence not perfect substitutes for one another).

The industry structure I call hollow middle, and which others including McKinsey often call balanced polarization, does not describe or reflect any degree of competition or lack thereof among providers in the industry, but looks at the industry structure from the perspective of *what clients want*. Essentially, there are three possibilities:

Migration to the high end. Here, people want a certain threshold and pretty high level of quality and reassurance about quality, or else they will purchase nothing at all. Think elective surgery, men's status watches (Rolex et al.), caviar, vintage wines, collectible art, digital SLR's, and to some extent even mass market products like smartphones. Industries like this have no room for generic or commodity producers, or indeed for any significant offerings at all that don't confer status, prestige, capability, or excellence.

Many goods and services that are deemed "superior" in the classic economic sense—meaning demand for them increases disproportionately as customers' income increases—occupy high-end migration industries. Possessing and displaying them, or talking about having experienced them in the case of services, connotes prestige almost per se.[50]

Migration to no frills/value. Here, people can't tell much difference among suppliers and so the cheapest and most economical—assuming only a bare minimum of baseline effectiveness and if applicable safety—will do. Such as? Retail groceries (we're passing by the organic goat's milk and the free-range brown eggs); desktop computers and servers; almost all office supplies; and to a degree dismaying and infuriating to the incumbent carriers, leisure air travel.

I wasn't being quite fair when I suggested people can't tell the difference; even the least frequent of frequent fliers among us probably could come up with a few words to distinguish American from Delta from United. But we really don't care when it's our money and a discretionary vacation trip— not if it means an additional 1% or 10% on the price.[51]

Lastly, the *hollow middle*. These industries—extremely common across the economy, about which I'll have more to say—are characterized by customers who sometimes will opt for the high end and sometimes will

---

50   For the vast bulk of goods and services, demand increases with income: That is to say, the income elasticity of demand is > 0. For superior goods, it's > 1. Another type of super-superior good, so-called "Veblen goods," may exist more in theory than in reality, but they would be goods for which a price decline would lower demand.

And yes, there are also "inferior" goods, demand for which increases as income *decreases* (their income elasticity of demand is < 0). Recognize that the label "inferior" has no reference whatsoever to these goods' quality: They adequately accomplish the purpose for which they were bought, but without flair or meaningful selection. "Inferior" simply refers to an empirically observable fact about the income distribution of consumers of these goods. Examples of inferior goods include everything from entry-level cars, inter-city bus service, payday loans, mobile homes, and bologna to shopping at dollar stores.

51   Objecting that a chasm separates the experience in coach from that in business, and that sometimes it's well worth paying to sit up front, misses the point: Those are tantamount to two separate products, priced, sold, and delivered separately. They're only the remotest substitutes for each other.

opt for economy, but see almost no value in offerings in-between. If our first example had suppliers clustered at the top of your mental chart, and our second at the bottom, this has two clusters more or less in the same places: With a lot of white space separating them.

What explains this bifurcated set of customer preferences? Simple; you've been there. In considering a host of goods to acquire or services to partake of, you want the high end quality or prestige experience some times, and the "sufficient," economical experience other times. *It depends.*

My surmise, unmoored to any data I could run down without torturing it into categories it wasn't gathered to fit, is that the majority of the economy by value—certainly for discretionary spending—is accounted for by industries with a hollow middle structure. Be that as it may, reflect for a moment on how you decide what you want in the following common categories. I'm guessing your thoughts bifurcate along lines similar to these:

- Clothing: the bespoke or designer suit, shirt, jacket, and slacks, or a polo and chinos from the Gap. Not an "OK" $50 dress shirt.

- Airlines (yes, them again): Southwest and RyanAir or Cathay Pacific and Singapore. Not America West, Braniff, Eastern, Frontier, National, Northwest, Pan Am, TWA, or etc.

- Cars: The Honda/Hyundai/Mazda/Nissan/Toyota econobox to get you through your commute or the Audi/BMW/Mercedes/Porsche/Tesla to give you a thrill. Not Plymouth, Pontiac, or Oldsmobile.

- Alcohol: Craft brew or Bud, waiting-list California cabernet or house chardonnay, 12-year single malt or the bar vodka.

- Jewelry: Costume or Tiffany/Cartier; Swatch/Fossil or Audemars Piguet/Patek Philippe.

- Financial services: Minimum fees checking from [indistinguishable convenient bank] or private client services from Credit Suisse, UBS, or Northern Trust.

You get the picture, and we needn't go on, but I think the last example may be the most instructive for Law Land. Financial services are surely more closely analogous to law than any of the other examples I just reeled off, and it displays a marvelously diverse and differentiated ecosystem of providers, with far more choice in terms of price, depth of product and service offerings, degree of intimacy and personalization, global reach or locally focused expertise, target customer base (check cashing outlets vs. Lazard Freres) and delivery channel—mail, phone, retail storefront (H&R Block) or branch (Bank of America, Chase, Citi, Wells Fargo), private office, online, and now app-based. Our imaginations seem impoverished by contrast.

What all these industry structures have in common is that, once a product or service category has reached equilibrium on almost any one of them (high, low, hollow middle), that structure tends to be extremely stable. It usually requires something tantamount to a Promethean spark to dislodge an industry from the equilibrium structure it has migrated into. Indeed, those occasions are so rare that they're ready-made for business school case studies and popular press admiration. Apple did it to music with iTunes but nobody's yet done it with TV, a number of online retailers are trying to do it with archaic categories (Warby Parker with eyeglasses, Casper and others with mattresses, Amazon with, well, who knows?). But barring revolutionary assaults, industries tend to settle into the form market evolution has pushed them towards.

If my hypothesis is right that clients in Law Land are increasingly viewing their law-firm selection process in terms of *"it depends,"* what might that portend?

Not much oxygen left for firms in the middle. In the wake of the Great Reset, we've seen clients bifurcate their spending and law firm selection decisions, sometimes pursuing a flight to quality and other times a flight to economy. Hollow middle firms benefit from neither. To clients, these firms may, with profoundly unfortunate consequences, represent simply the generic law firm, providing a one-size-fits-all level of expertise, a destination for nothing in particular, jack of all trades and master of none.

Why patronize such a firm? What is distinctive about them? Why choose them over a firm down the block or across town? If your clients can't answer that, you should be worried. If you can't answer that, you should be alarmed.

Finally, the **Integrated Focus** crowd. This is my own perhaps ill-advised coinage as in the time since *Taxonomy* was published it seems to have provoked more perplexity than any other category.

What these firms have in common is actually quite simple: They are designed and built around an *external* client or industry orientation, not internal law-firm-centric suppositions. So instead of assuming that any proper law firm needs corporate/transactional capability, with or without a smattering of M&A, public company work, and other satellite practices; and dispute resolution/litigation; and one or more of labor and employment; T&E; real estate; tax; etc...., the firm looks to what client base or industry coverage it wants to specialize in and designs services specific to that and only that market orientation.

To provide examples and name names, Proskauer and Wilson Sonsini were often nominated by readers as integrated focus firms—Proskauer for serving the non-bank sector of financial services, and Wilson Sonsini for of course tech-centric startups and young companies primarily out of Silicon Valley. For purposes of discussion, let's stipulate this is a large part of what these firms do.

Now ask yourself whether Wilson Sonsini needs a substantial real estate practice? Pretty obviously not.[52] Or whether Proskauer needs a banking practice? Same.[53]

What it takes to be an integrated focus is easy to state—design your firm to serve your target market—and apparently diabolically difficult to carry out, at least if one believes there's a reason that this category attracted fewer firms as nominees than any of the other six business models. Perhaps it has to do with the mandatory discipline within integrated focus firms of being able to say "no"—no to clients who'd like you to help them with something peripheral, no to partners panting to bring in a large non-core

---

52   At publication, the firm's website listed four partners under real estate, one of them retired: https://wsgr.com/WSGR/DBIndex.aspx?SectionName=attorneys/results.htm

53   On the "Practices" page for Proskauer, the words "bank" and "banking" don't appear at all. This for a firm whose corporate department has 25% more lawyers than any other single practice area. http://www.proskauer.com/practices/

client or matter, no to otherwise perfect laterals who would fall outside your self-imposed practice area lines.

Being serious about the integrated focus design also requires you to step away from this common diagrammatic view of the law firm solar system, where the firm is at the center and the elements of its supply (talent and services) and demand (clients) revolve around it:

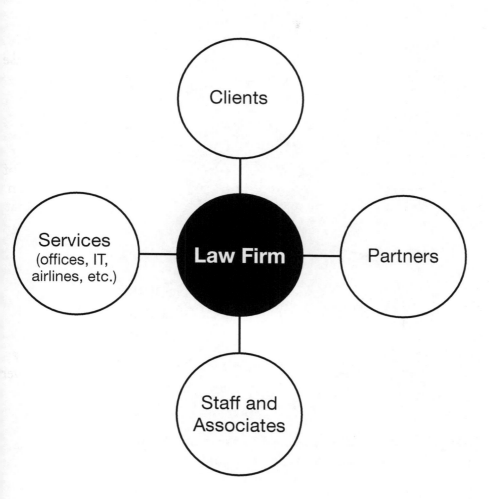

Instead, you need to put the client at the center, and realize that the client has options for supplying its demand for legal services, including, yes, law firms, but also technology, contract services, the Big Four accountancies, and even "doing without," which is often a plausible substitute where conventional approaches are simply too expensive to justify:

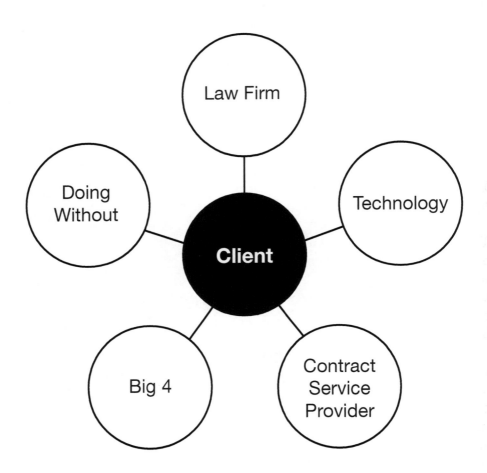

Integrated focus firms realize clients have many options and design themselves to be attractive to their target market.

Summing Up

As you know:

- None of these law firm business models is foolproof; there are exceptional and awful examples of firms in each category.

- Firms are not sentenced to perpetual stasis in whichever category they currently find themselves in; change and evolution are possible.

- And finally: These seven categories I introduced a few years ago are not exhaustive and not exclusive. For example, I do not anywhere here address the plaintiffs' bar or solo and small-town practitioners.

You are utterly at liberty to invent your own category and design a firm to occupy it.

The point is to choose a direction and a desired goal and pursue it with disciplined seriousness and steeliness of purpose until you arrive or realize the market is telling you that you would be well advised to come up with a Plan B. (I told you there's no guarantee of success and no sentence to failure; this holds true for categories beyond those enumerated in *Taxonomy*.)

I can assure you that trying to be all things to all people, or letting go of the tiller and letting the prevailing winds guide you, or lacking the courage the say 'no,' or indulging in the childish faith that nostalgia is a strategy, will condemn you to the market's judgment that you are irrelevant and extraneous. And when I say "the market's" judgment, I mean the considered stance of clients and talent, the air and water of a law firm.

You are at liberty to tack towards irrelevance; no natural law of economics, finance, or human nature prohibits you. I've tried to provide examples of the varieties of decisions firms can make to avoid that fate. But the choice is entirely, and continually, yours.

"Business models can't change. Once a business learns how to make money one way, it's almost impossible to shift gears. But there is one slender reed of hope: While businesses can't change, firms can."

—Tom Bartman, Senior Researcher, Harvard Business School's Christensen Forum for Growth and Innovation.

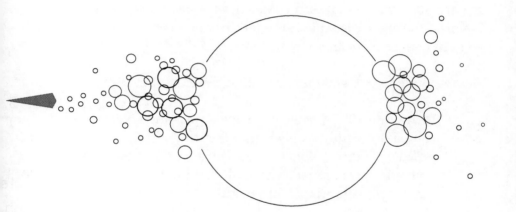

New Entrants Win

In *The Innovator's Dilemma,* [54] Clayton Christensen popularized, probably beyond his wildest dreams, the phenomenon of new entrants to an established industry disrupting it from below, as it were, by introducing relatively primitive products with miserly features—but that are inexpensive—that initially fly beneath the radar of entrenched incumbents and seem to pose no competitive threat to the prevailing offerings with lavish features supported by rich distribution networks, superb customer service, and an installed base with a substantial history behind it.

We *cognoscenti* now know how this story ends. The Neanderthal incumbents ignore the rough and tumble upstarts at their peril, dismissing them (if they pay attention at all) as offering substandard products which no self-respecting customer would have any interest in. Until it's too late and digital photography engulfs Kodak, the supermarket destroys the mighty A&P (which in its intra-Wars heyday was equivalent in size to Walmart today), the Japanese auto industry neutron-bombs Detroit, and you can be sure there are more to come.

Here's a quite recent, and quite poignant, report from the trenches.[55]

> In autumn 2007, Jorma Ollila, the chairman of Nokia, polled 12 top company executives on whether they thought Apple's new iPhone posed a big threat. Two said no, Ollila recalls in "Against All Odds," a surprisingly engrossing memoir first published in Finland in 2013 but just now translated into English.
>
> The other ten thought the iPhone would prove a serious competitor that we shouldn't underestimate. Some of them expressed their views in terms not fit for publication. The message was clear: **most of Nokia's key people were alert enough to grasp that Apple really had thrown down the gauntlet in the contest for the smartphone market.**

---

54   Properly, *The Innovator's Dilemma: When New Technologies Cause Great Firms to Fail,* Harvard Business Press (Cambridge: 1997). I've always thought that the more apt title would have been "The Incumbent's Dilemma," but Professor Christensen neglected to consult me in advance.

55   Justin Fox, *Why Nokia Couldn't Beat the iPhone,* 18 October 2016, Bloomberg View, at: https://www.bloomberg.com/view/articles/2016-10-18/why-nokia-couldn-t-beat-the-iphone (bold emphasis supplied)

The subtitle of Ollila's book is "Leading Nokia from Near Catastrophe to Global Success," and the story of the company's transformation from failing Finnish conglomerate when he took over as CEO in 1992 to global mobile-phone juggernaut by decade's end really is pretty amazing.

But so is the story of what happened after 2007, as Nokia's market share collapsed and it finally sold the phone business to Microsoft, which is now shutting much of it down. He does not shy, in print or in person, from addressing the calamitous change in Nokia's fortunes. **His overriding message is that, even when you recognize an existential threat to your company, it can be really hard to get out of the way.**

Nokia's leadership knew since at least 2004 that smartphones were probably the future of mobile, and that operating-system software was the key competitive differentiator. The company had even been selling a pioneering smartphone, the Communicator, since 1996. But when Apple -- followed by Google and Microsoft -- set to work building operating systems for phones, Nokia just couldn't keep up.

> "The computer industry heritage and operating-system know-how on the West Coast of the U.S. was just too much. That was the main reason."

Reason No. 2 was that it's really hard to shift the direction of a giant, heretofore spectacularly successful organization.

From the book:

> "We understood the problem, but at some deep level we couldn't accept what was happening. Many big projects just carried on. We examined the sales projections for the following quarter, when our eyes should have been focused much further ahead."

And:

> "The worst that can happen to a company is to run out of money and be forced into bankruptcy. **Enormous success is perhaps the next worst.**"

> For all the attention lavished over the past 20 years on the threat of disruptive innovation and how established companies should respond to it, I don't think established companies have gotten much better at it. Maybe they just *can't*.

"They just can't" is probably an overstatement, but the diabolical insight at the heart of Christensen's model was not that the incumbents were being obtuse and blind, or pig-headed and greedy, but that they were behaving perfectly rationally by redoubling their focus on serving their existing customers better than ever in light of the new competition.

To paraphrase a key part of his argument, the incumbent's most important customers have no use at the moment for the new technology and, therefore, show little interest in it. Rationally, established firms believe their strongest defense against the upstart is to double down on the pace of investing in their existing ways of doing things. They do this in order to keep up with the needs of their current customers and thereby win the competitive wars against their familiar peer set of established firms— which can play that very same game on that very same board.

This aspect of Christensen's theory is too often overlooked in the version that has come down to us in popular thinking: Not that the maladroit incumbents deserved to lose, but that in a very sympathetic sense they had little choice but to keep doing what they did best.

> "[M]anaging better, working harder, and not making so many dumb mistakes is not the answer to the innovator's dilemma. […]

> Despite their endowments in technology, brand names, manufacturing prowess, management experience, distribution muscle, and just plain cash, successful companies populated by

good managers have a genuinely hard time doing what does not fit their model for how to make money. Because disruptive [entrants] rarely make sense during the years when investing in them is most important, conventional managerial wisdom at established firms constitutes an entry and mobility barrier that entrepreneurs and investors can bank on. It is powerful and pervasive."[56]

Arnold Toynbee (1889—1975) was one of the most prominent historians of the 20th Century and a professor for most of is career at the London School of Economics. His majestic life work was the 12-volume *Study of History* (published from 1934 to 1961) examined the rise and fall of 26 civilizations throughout human history and concluded that the key reason all ultimately failed boiled down to this toxic dynamic:

> When a civilization responded to challenges, it grew. Civilizations declined when their leaders stopped responding creatively, and the civilizations then sank owing to nationalism, militarism, and the tyranny of a despotic minority.[57]

Or, as Toynbee himself more pithily summarized his ultimate conclusion:

> "Nothing fails like success."

Contrast that with this declaration delivered by the managing partner of an AmLaw 25 firm on a panel of experts at a symposium in New York in late 2016:

> "One can always increase one's level of prudence and caution."

Then of course there are a host of counterfactuals to Christensen's paradigm where the incumbents successfully fought the upstarts into submission. As of 2016, we have ringside seats to what could shape up to be one of the biggest, baddest, most bruising battles for the soul of an industry in recent business history: The fight for the future of the car/truck/vehicle transportation market. The timing coincidence of the all but simultaneous arrival of the first real world electric cars in over a century,

---

56   *Innovator's Dilemma,* HarperCollins Business, 2011 reprint edition (New York) at 257, 260—261.

57   Arnold Toynbee, Wikipedia, at: https://en.wikipedia.org/wiki/Arnold_J._Toynbee

and driverless technologies, has opened up this industry to competition on a scale unthinkable just five or ten years ago.

What's particularly riveting about this war isn't just the global stakes, although they're huge,[58] but the fascinatingly different approaches being taken to Tesla's electric platform challenge by GM (the all-electric Bolt), Toyota (perhaps the industry's highest profile brand line in this area, Prius), BMW (the futuristic i-X series including the $150,000, 0—60 mph in < 4 seconds i8 supercar), Mercedes Benz (apparently learning with relatively small, moderate-performance models), and other incumbents.

Meanwhile over in the driverless technology theater, Tesla, Google, Apple, Ford, Volvo, Mercedes Benz and others all seem to be striking out in different directions of their own. This isn't a book about driverless vehicles' likely adoption curve, but one could do worse than reflect for a moment on the core challenge all these companies are facing: The human-computer interface, or, at critical moments, the "handoff" from machine to man when extreme situations arise.

Logic would suggest that incumbents, with (in the case of Law Land) their cadres of sophisticated professionals, established client relations, profound domain expertise, and healthy cash flows, would possess ample resources to devote to fighting off challengers.

At the least in theory this is correct. Consider the options law firms have. Imitating upstarts and essentially stealing their thunder by doing more or less what the upstarts do but under a Big Law brand umbrella. This seems to be at least part of what Allen & Overy's PeerPoint service is achieving: Providing an equivalently cost-effective and inexpensive labor market arbitrage alternative to the Axiom's of the world, but with the reassuring imprimatur of Allen & Overy standing behind it.

The inevitable and profoundly unimaginative objective from within the law firm will be anticipated: Why should we charge such low rates for work we were charging such high rates for last year? For most any law firm, at

---

58   According to US Bureau of Labor Statistics data, vehicle sales and service accounts for about 5.5% of GDP. (The series I'm using is in a dataset called "GDPbyInd_VA_1947-2015.xlsx.") If you assume a current US GDP of approximately $17.5-trillion, this would indicate vehicle sales and service at ~$963 billion, or $1-trillion as an order of magnitude.

least for now, this is a show-stopper and would shut down any proposal to create (say) a Cravath or Davis Polk version of PeerPoint.

Why Allen & Overy was able to do so was described succinctly by David Morley, the firm's Senior Partner [Chairman and CEO] at the time, who was asked his response to the "cannibalizing ourselves" objection at a conference I attended in New York in late 2015: "The answer is that if we don't do it to ourselves, someone else will do it to us. That objection has actually stopped coming up." Spoken as a true market Darwinist.

And other firms to be sure, are flocking towards some version of performing the labor market arbitrage gavotte internally with offshore, onshore, or near-shore locations. Orrick showed the way nearly 15 year ago when it opened its "Global Operations Center" in Wheeling, West Virginia, and the list of followers continues to grow including WilmerHale (Dayton, OH), Freshfields (Manchester), Ashurst (Glasgow), and many others, some of whom I know to be doing it in stealth mode by taking advantage of kinder and gentler cost of living jurisdictions where they already have existing offices.

• • •

We need to step back for a moment and discuss exactly what type of business model our putative new entrant friends are following.

So far I've made it look easy for Big Law to fight back if all the new entrants offer is what I've summarily characterized as labor market arbitrage. This is a thoroughly understood business model, with zero meaningful barriers to entry. Indeed, calling it a business model is almost grand; it's really just proper operational hygiene.

Proof positive that it's hygiene and not a full-blown differentiating model in its own right is that it provides no sustainable competitive advantage to the firms adopting it. They may feel they're running faster, but all they've achieved is avoiding losing ground. It's essentially a defensive and protective measure. This is the evil twin to "no barriers to entry."

Two types of new entrants we already see in the market follow business models that are truly, fundamentally, distinct from Law Land, and that's why I find them of great interest. The first, what I'll call "Type 1" new entrants, are new entrants to Law Land but hardly new entrants to markets: The Big Four accounting firms.

"Type 2" new entrants are what I'll call firms that are reconceiving how legal services are performed starting with a clean sheet of paper. This is harder than it sounds, and you can lay most of the blame for how challenging it is at how hard we find it to discard assumptions accumulated over the course of a professional career.

It's no coincidence that many of these Type 2 firms are being led by people whose previous background and experience had nothing to do with Law. This fresh perspective inspires intellectual and conceptual creativity, we can be sure, but also—and this may be more powerful for being subtler—means they feel no emotional or sentimental ties to law Land.

I've never actually heard any of them say this, but it could hardly be more obvious that they have no fear of—and many have molten ambition to—break some china. They all live by the same motto that helped Jeff Bezos take Amazon as far as it has gotten in challenging conventional retailers, warehouse and fulfillment services, cloud computing platforms, and who-knows-what-next (FedEx, UPS, and the US Postal Service?):

"Your margin is my opportunity."

Type 1: The Big Four

The Big Four are hardly hiding their ambitions for Law Land under a bushel. Here's just a sampling of recent news:

- Revenue at PwC Legal in the UK grew 25% from £48.5M to £59.9M in the fiscal year ending in 2016, yielding £11M in profits (slightly over an 18% profit margin).

- EY's global law practice has 1,500 legal professionals in 67 countries

- Deloitte Legal also has global ambitions, with (again) over 1,500 professionals in more than 70 countries

- KPMG Legal offers advice across the globe in corporate restructuring, contract review and drafting, employment, regulation, immigration, tax, and global corporate secretarial.

A few more data points:

- Last year about 5—10% of US law school graduates went to work for an accounting firm;

- PwC, EY, and KPMG have all secured ABS licenses in the UK; only Deloitte has, to date, demurred;

- PwC has announced publicly its intent to grow its legal services revenue to $1-billion by 2019 (closer than you think), which would make it an AmLaw 20-size provider;

- And all three of the firms currently active have made some high-profile hires, including practice heads in areas including finance, corporate, project finance, and private equity, from firms such as Addleshaw Goddard, Baker & McKenzie, Berwin Leighton Paisner, DLA, Freshfields, McDermott Will & Emery, Olswang, and Weil Gotshal.

And they have resources in spades: The combined revenue of the Big Four is substantially greater than that of the AmLaw 200—as of 2015 (latest figures available at publication) about $150 billion for the Big Four combined vs. just barely north of $100-billion for the AmLaw firms.

In terms of headcount, there is no public data on the AmLaw 200, but we can estimate that if the typical lawyer:staff ratio at such firms is 1:1, the 121,918 lawyers (according to the 2016 *The AmLaw 200*) at those firms would yield an informed guess of slightly under 250,000 total professionals and staff.

Meanwhile, the *smallest* of the Big Four (KPMG) employs 173,965 worldwide and the largest (Deloitte) 225,351. The total, with EY at 211,450 and PwC at 208,109, is 818,875.[59]

---

59   *Number of employees of the Big Four accounting/audit firms worldwide in 2015,* Statista.com, https://www.statista.com/statistics/250503/big-four-accounting-firms-number-of-employees/

Any of the Big Four has a local presence on the ground in vastly more markets than any even the most far-flung of the AmLaw 200: Consider these growth rates over just three years:[60]

Number of Countries where legal services are offered	2012	2015	% of countries outside Europe (2015)
PWC	70	85	55%
Deloitte	49	69	51%
KPMG	39	53	36%
EY	23	69	49%

The Big Four are in, or could gain immediate entrée to, essentially every Fortune 1000 and FTSE 250 boardroom, whether through the doors called audit or tax or consulting; their brands' market recognition is at saturation levels. Deloitte alone has 5,000 "client service representatives," each assigned to one or more corporations, whose full-time job is to introduce and sell Deloitte products and services to their client base. Not irrationally, their compensation depends on the value of what they can persuade their clients to buy, but they're rewarded for anything and everything clients purchase that has the Deloitte brand on it—including "Deloitte Legal."

Contrast this with the business development model of Law Land: For all but the rarest and most elite firms, the amount of revenue partners can generate, their so-called "client origination," is a key component of determining compensation.[61] Superficially this resembles the Deloitte system, but in reality and in terms of incentives it could not be more different.

At the vast majority of firms, it's in partners' individual self-interest to hoard client relationships or at least hoard responsibility for individual matters. Sharing origination credit, matter management responsibility,

---

60   David Wilkins and Maria Jose Esteban, *The Role of the Big Four Accountancy Firms in the Reconfiguration of the Global Market for Legal Services,* Harvard Law School Center on the Legal Profession, Working Paper 2016-01.

61   I have yet to encounter a firm where origination credit is calculated on the profitability of the work generated as opposed to the sheer throw-weight of gross revenue brought in the door, but that's a topic for another day.

nd actual billable work may get lip service from management in the name
f encouraging "firm-wide collaboration" and "delivering the best lawyer
1 the firm for the client," but at year-end compensation time most systems
illy up everyone's statistics and those who generously gave away clients,
natters, responsibility, and hours are penalized in the wallet. Not so with
)eloitte's client service representatives: They deliver everything Deloitte
as to offer to their clients and are rewarded for anything and everything
nder the Deloitte brand.[62]

Iost importantly, as corporations, the Big Four have the luxury, or at least
he discretionary opportunity, to invest retained earnings. When one of
hem chooses to target an industry or a market vertical, they can and have
ssigned as many as 10,000 professionals to a massive year-long project
ɔ build up process maps, workflow diagrams, detailed contact databases,
nalytic tools, reservoirs of thoughtful backgrounders and whitepapers,
nd so forth, and to build a deep and rich resource in thought leadership.
Jote that being assigned to such a project is not viewed as being put on an
xtraneous or peripheral sidetrack in the least, but is in fact a desirable and
ven sought-after part of one's career path—akin to an American being
emporarily posted abroad or a rotation through finance for a non-quant.

---

2   Another powerful incentive for partners to hoard client relationships in Law Land
is to keep their books of business "portable" to maximize their market value in the event
hey choose to decamp to another firm. While this is less obviously the "fault" of the
aw firm than are the unintended but utterly foreseeable consequences of compensation
ystems driven by individual productivity, it has no counterpart whatsoever among the
Big Four, where clients are institutional clients of The Firm and client teams are regularly
ɔtated on a mandatory schedule with new senior, mid-level, and junior consultants being
ntroduced to the client to maintain continuity and reinforce the perception and the reality
hat allegiances run between the corporate client and the Big Four firm itself, not between
he the corporate client and whatever individual happens to be the relationship manager
hat year.

Vhy couldn't more law firms broadly emulate this model? (Most of the super-elite,
predominantly lockstep-driven firms already do, but as always they're the exception,
ot the Law Land rule.) This question has long troubled me, since it seems so obviously
uperior as a standard, rational part of the how a professional services business should
perate. The answer may simply arise from reality on the ground, not thoughtful
eflection. I think the hypothesis with the greatest explanatory power has to do with raw
power rather than theories of the optimal business model. The more business a partner
s generating—the bigger a rainmaker they are—the less likely firm leadership is to
hallenge them on, well, on almost anything (including antisocial behavior sometimes up
ɔ and sometimes beyond arguably actionable harassment).

But the distinction between clients of the institution and those of a lone wolf is quite real.
ndeed, lateral partners coming out of those super-elite lockstep firms are only in demand
by other firms who really need their skillsets and capabilities, because those individuals
ire notorious for being able to bring no meaningful business with them.

These professionals are then plunged back into client relations when the assault on the targeted vertical launches.

The question answers itself, but imagine a law firm assigning 10% of its lawyers to such a project for a year while cutting them off from client practice. "Business models can't change." No, indeed.

At about this point some of you may be thinking that we in the US have the lifeline of prohibitions on what non-lawyers can do to protect us. Sure the UK has the 2007 Legal Services Act, which virtually rolls out the red carpet for the Big Four, but "not going to happen here."

Let's review how we in the US got here. In the 1990's, the then-Big 5 set up quasi-independent legal networks operating under the brand of the accounting firms that were designed to resemble traditional law firms as much as possible, together with marketing and public relations campaigns communicating the message that they were like any top law firm, only bigger. Four of the five—Andersen Legal, Landwell, KLegal, and E&Y Law—achieved scale equal to or surpassing the larges taw firms.

We all know what happened next. After Arthur Andersen ended up being indicted in the wake of the Enron scandal and was forced to dissolve, taking Andersen Legal with it, the tide of regulation flowed in and Sarbanes-Oxley purported to ban accountancies from providing non-audit services to audit clients. Approximately none of the rhetoric surrounding these events noted that Andersen Legal had nothing whatsoever to do with Enron. No matter. Andersen Legal was hit by a stray bullet, and the others were shuttered along with it.

During the past decade or so, the Big Four have been playing the game differently—quietly and inconspicuously. Being able to start with a clean sheet of paper, they have built legal organizations designed around where the 21st Century appears to be going. Specifically:

- They're heavier in Asia-Pacific, Latin America, Africa, and the Middle East than traditional law firms;

- They're organized as matrix models, offering not just legal expertise but alongside it deep industry knowledge, big-data analytics, and their classic compliance and risk management know-how; and

- None too soon, they've shown they recognize the need to pay up for top talent.

Finally and perhaps most importantly, each of the four has been pursuing long-term and disciplined strategies of diversifying their revenue and client base out of commoditized auditing services. Non-audit clients now provide the majority of each of the four firms' revenue. With the global legal services market projected to total $726.6-billion in 2019,[63] the Big Four are intensely focused on it. Even a 1% market share for any one of them would make that network the largest legal services provider in the world.

US-based law firms may still point to Sarbanes-Oxley as their castle and their moat, but I beg to differ.

I believe it is inevitably in the cards not just thanks to the dynamics of markets—"don't fight the tape" is an old Wall Street mantra, embedding the almost irresistible tendency for markets to have their way—but also thanks to what we know about the history of social-policy and judicial challenges to guild restrictions on qualifications for entrance and the "unauthorized practice" of X, Y, Z.

First, note that pretty much every successful challenge to guild restrictions has been based on a combination of antitrust, commerce-clause, and free speech. This was true of the 1977 *Bates* decision permitting lawyer advertising and was the genesis of the UK's Clementi Commission itself, which led to the LSA. Second, how many of you noted the Supreme Court's February 2015 decision in **North Carolina State Board of Dental Examiners vs. FTC (2015)**?[64] In summary it upheld the FTC's challenge to the North Carolina dental licensing board's practice of excluding non-dentists from the market for teeth whitening—as anticompetitive and an unfair restraint of trade.

Of particular note are these lines:

The Court has rejected the argument that it would be unwise to apply the antitrust laws to professional regulation [absent extenuating

---

63   Id.

64   https://www.supremecourt.gov/opinions/14pdf/13-534_19m2.pdf

circumstances and] particularly in light of the risks licensing boards dominated by market participants may pose to the free market.

So if a challenge to The Rules of Professional Conduct's prohibition on non-lawyer ownership were either brought by (say) a Big Four, or conversely if an action to prohibit (say) a Big Four from providing "lawyerly" services were brought by a lawyer or law firm, my money would be on the prohibition falling.

Type 2: New new entrants

In emerging areas where, to be honest, none of us can predict what's actually going to happen, I decided to provide a series of profiles or mini-case studies if you will, about three exemplar firms in an attempt to demonstrate how varied are the approaches to attacking the beast called the global legal services market. All they have in common is that they're (a) new (b) come with intrinsic barriers to entry, or at least to fast following, and (c) are firms I have previously come across in my travels.

I invite you not to suspend your critical faculties, which would be antithetical to the way I approach the world, but to dial them down from the "judgment and sentence" Level 10 to the "listen and ponder" Level 4.

Without further ado:

• • •

Novus Law

Ray Bayley and Lois Haubold, neither a lawyer and neither with previous experience in Law Land, founded Novus Law a little over ten years ago

1 2005.[65] They had begun examining legal processes and concluded in
short order that they were remarkably inefficient—a realization they
quickly discovered few in Law Land shared—and believed the industry was
overdue for positive, yet radical change.

Novus is based in Chicago, Illinois, , employs more than a hundred
professionals worldwide, and has grown to annual revenues on the order
of $20 to $25M. It has long been cash-flow positive and profitable. It
received a small round of friends and family funding when it began and
has self-funded all of its growth since.

A defining principle for Novus, and part of Ray and Lois' management
philosophy, is to organize the delivery of services around processes, not
functions. This may sound mysterious to the uninitiated but it has a
well-recognized and mainstream pedigree in management literature,
most famously elaborated in Michael Hammer and James Champy's
Reengineering the Corporation: A manifesto for business revolution,[66] which
was called "the most important business book of its decade."

Reengineering focuses on defining what products or services a business
(a law firm) must supply to its customers and then digs into the details of
how best to supply them in order to optimize the processes involved. Let
me recount an early "a-ha!" moment in the life of Novus and then explain
how reengineering applies to put the insight gained in that instant into an
ongoing business.[67]

---

65   Ray, President, CEO, and Co-Founder, previously was Managing Partner of
PricewaterhouseCoopers' North American Business Process Outsourcing organization,
one of the leading outsourcing organizations in the world, and was a member of the firm's
5-member management committee, responsible for overseeing the US operations of
the firm comprising 70,000 people and $9 billion in revenue. He earned his B.S. from the
University of Illinois and MBA from Northwestern's Kellogg School.

Lois, Executive Vice President and Co-Founder, is responsible for the firm's strategy,
ethics, global service delivery, and client relations. Previously she was part of the
leadership team of PricewaterhouseCoopers' North American Business Process
Outsourcing group. She received B.S. and M.S. degrees from the University of Illinois
and an MBA from Northwestern's Kellogg School.

have known both Ray and Lois well for some time.

66   Harper Collins: New York, 1st ed. 1993, 2d ed. 2003.

67   Interview with Ray and Lois, November 2016, paraphrased for
clarity and concision.

Our first client ever was a biotech startup, represented by Kirkland & Ellis. The company was in a do-or-die lawsuit with a markedly superior drug about to exit trials and launch. If successful, they would destroy the market share of a large biotech that was suing to block its release. We went through the drill of electronically tagging [roughly speaking, indexing] and organizing gigabytes of our client's documents, a process known as first-level document review and turned them back over to Kirkland.

What was at stake was simple: The CEO of our client had to decide whether to raise new capital to defend the lawsuit or roll over and give up. Since the CEO knew we'd completed our review, he called us and asked, "Now that you've read all of my documents, what happened?"

We didn't know what the answer was at that point and even though the law firm had all the documents meticulously tagged and organized, neither did they. Once we turned over the documents to the law firm, they immediately set about reading and re-reading them all over again to see what happened – a process that would take many more months – a process we call "the traditional process."

That was the moment we realized that what clients really wanted was not tagged and organized documents but the answer to the question, "What's the story?" Tagging documents, or doing first-level document review, was akin to selling a drill to our client when all they really wanted was the hole, or in this case, the story.

Ever since that happened ten years ago, Novus has focused on finding the story – or, if the documents could talk, what story would they tell?

This changes everything. Novus focuses on finding, documenting and delivering the story from the very first document they review instead of tagging and organizing documents, which then will simply have to be read and re-read in multiple stages.

before proceeding further, permit me to explain "read and re-read at every stage." The way Law Land is currently arranged is into silo'ed verticals: Companies responsible for e-discovery, contract lawyers, LPO's, law firms (which are themselves silo'ed into submarkets of junior and senior associates, and partners). When matters pass from one silo to another— say from an LPO to a law firm—the new silo has to start all over by re-reading the documents to learn the matter and much of what was learned in the last reading is lost. The cost of doing this reading and re-reading is tremendous. Let's assume the average billing rate to do this work across an LPO and all of the law firm silos is $360 per hour, or $6 per minute or $3 per page, assuming a lawyer reads two pages per minute, which is typical.

When you read and re-read documents multiple times at a rate of $3 per page or $15 per document the costs really add up, making this the largest and fastest growing revenue generator for Law Land and largest and fastest growing legal expense for clients. The friction involved is also tremendous, and tremendously costly. Economists, including yours truly, are not fans of transaction costs and friction, and here Novus had identified a glaring systemic source of those very expenses in the traditional process.

Now, it might be one thing if reading and re-reading (and re-reading and…) documents added only cost and expense, but it's worse than that; it introduces and compounds errors, a/k/a "defects" into the document examination process. This runs so profoundly counter to the way lawyers instinctively think about checking and reviewing others' work—"it's an intrinsic part of how our firm guarantees quality!"—that it begs for explanation.

Consider a simple e-discovery or due diligence document-sorting project. The goal of the examiners is to categorize documents as (a) not relevant or not germane—we can assume the vast majority; (b) responsive or germane; and (c) privileged and/or confidential—which doesn't really have an analog in the case of transactional review due diligence.[68] And

---

68   Although the concepts of lawyer confidentiality, attorney-client privilege, and work product protection are technically distinct, it's immaterial to our discussion of Novus Law. (See Sue Michmerhuizen, *Confidentiality, Privilege: A Basic Value in Two Different Applications,* American Bar Association: May, 2007 at http://www.americanbar.org/content/dam/aba/administrative/professional_responsibility/confidentiality_or_attorney.authcheckdam.pdf).

let's make the perhaps heroic assumption that our examiners achieve 97% accuracy. That means that 3% of the documents are mis-coded on the first pass.

So let's go to our de rigueur "second review," also 97% accurate, and see what happens. What's *supposed to happen* is that the 3% that were miscoded are corrected so that we have achieved [(97%) + (97% x 3% = 2.91%)] = 99.91% accuracy.

But in the real world that's not what happens at all. The premise of the second review is that no one knows going in which documents constitute the "3%" and which are the "97%;" after all, if we knew that we would have corrected the 3% on the spot, as part of the first review. So we re-review all of them, with the result that after the second review the accuracy drops from 97% to 94.1% (97% x 97% = 94.1%). Do you still plan to engage in a third review? It will take you to 91.3% accurate, for the record. Do the overall math and the results aren't pretty; when you read and re-read documents multiple times as is done in the traditional process, the costs are exorbitant and the quality is poor, even if everyone who examines a document is 99% accurate.

Now let's go back to "reengineering" and what it actually means in the context of a business like Law Land.

Reengineering begins from the premise that most business processes are fragmented into a series of component functions, and that those functions are poorly and arbitrarily connected, creating friction and excess costs. Reengineering breaks apart the process, leading to the creation of the product or service (here, "the story the documents tell") into its component parts and reconfigures them in a blank-sheet-of-paper fashion. Often entire sub-functions, it's discovered, can be disposed of.

Another tenet of reengineering is that one centralized decision point needs to manage the entire process, and be accountable for results. No more of the Dilbert-ian buck-passing where design hands it to engineering which hands it to operations which hands it to production which hands

t to sales and marketing, at the end of which the product/service is an
unrecognizable (and unsatisfactory) camel.[69]

The core difference between reengineering and incremental efficiencies
s this:

> This drive for realizing dramatic improvements by fundamentally
> re-thinking how the organization's work should be done
> distinguishes the re-engineering from process improvement efforts
> that focus on functional or incremental improvement.[70]

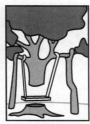

| How the customer explained it | How the project leader understood it | How the engineer designed it | How the programmer wrote it | How the sales executive described it |

| How the project was documented | What opreations installed | How the customer was billed | How the help desk supported it | What the customer really needed |

---

69   The famous "tire swing" cartoon has been around in various iterations since
at least the early 1960's; the earliest documented example came from an internal
newsletter circulated among the British Civil Service called, fittingly, *Red Tape:* See
Tree Swing Pictures, Businessballs.com (undated) at http://www.businessballs.com/
treeswing.htm. It has been in the public domain since at least the 1970's. For those of
you not familiar with it, here's a rather advanced rendition (from Jewel Ward, *The Project
Management Tree Swing Cartoon, Past and Present,* <tamingdata />, August 7, 2010, at:
http://www.tamingdata.com/2010/07/08/the-project-management-tree-swing-cartoon-
past-and-present/)

70   United States GAO, *Business Process Reengineering Assessment Guide,* May
1997, at: http://www.gao.gov/assets/80/76302.pdf

Ray describes how this has changed what Novus does:

> Now, if we start looking at documents at 8:00 am Monday, we're
> producing usable work product (the beginnings of the story) by
> 8:15 or 8:30 and if a client logs on to the Novus system in 24 hours
> or a week later, the client and the law firm can figure out basically
> what's going on.[71]

"What's the goal?" I ask. "To distill 2 million documents into 2,000
words in a matter of days rather than the months it typically takes to
find the story."

Lawyers still, by and large, write those stories, but people with journalism
backgrounds are also on staff and everyone gets regular in-house training
on writing. Not just legal writing: investigative journalism writing. How
do we report the facts without opinion but let it still be a compelling
read, as it would come out in summation to a jury or a motion for
summary judgment?

Don't kid yourself into thinking that this is just a snappier way to get to
"the story." It has much more far-reaching implications, deriving from the
powerful economics of information asymmetry: The Novus client and that
client's law firm know what the story is a long time before the opposing
party does. If the story that's emerging is a big bad scary story, wouldn't
you want to know that and strike a settlement accordingly? Or if the story
is nothing's really here, then you also know what to do.

Do not, again, kid yourself that what Novus has achieved is simple or that
you could clone it at the drop of a hat. The Novus Process™ actually has
three inter-related components:

- Novus One-Touch attacks the perils of reading and re-reading
  documents at their root, by using the Lean Manufacturing principles
  of Toyota to eliminate the tens or hundreds of wasteful and
  excessively expensive "touches" involved in the traditional process
  of reading and re-reading documents to find the story and reducing
  them to one touch per document for every purpose: Building the

---

71   "Work product" means identification of the hot or key documents on which the
case will turn; analysis and summary of which witnesses know what, when; and analysis
and summary of the key themes in the case – all together, the story.

story and categorizing documents accurately (more than 99.9% accurate, according to independent, statistically valid audits conducted by clients' law firms).[72]

- Novus Q is one of at most a handful of ISO 9001:2015 certified quality management programs in the global legal profession. You don't need to know everything ISO 9001:2008 requires to understand how rigorous it is, but suffice to say among other things it uses the Six Sigma principles created by Motorola and made famous by Jack Welch at GE to eliminate the mistakes that are unavoidable using the traditional process used to read and re-read documents.

- Novus C[3] harnesses the collective intelligence of everyone working on a matter ("the wisdom of crowds," in the vernacular) to eradicate the cognitive bias of individuals and ensure every story told is complete and precise. (C[3] is a Novus coinage standing for an online matter-specific application in which Novus' clients, their law firms, and Novus professionals all work together in one virtual place to communicate, collaborate, and control matters.)

Using the Novus Process, Novus has proven to reduce overall legal fees 25 to 35 percent, according to Deanna Johnston, the former vice president of litigation at Fireman's Fund Insurance Company, with whom Novus received an Association of Corporate Counsel Value Champion Award. According to Ray, that's a $3 to $4 reduction in law firm fees using the Novus Process for each $1 billed by Novus.

If Novus is the better mousetrap, why isn't it—or its competitive fast-following clones—more widely known and more widely adopted? I asked Ray this:

> When people try to understand what Novus does, they often ask if we compete against Axiom or against Pangaea 3 or against law firms, and the answer is that we compete against some of them on some things some of the time and against none of them. More fundamentally, we've created a niche that we occupy ourselves, doing away with the functional view of how work is traditionally done and focusing on process.

---

72   See generally *The Novus Approach*, undated, at http://novuslaw.com/approach/

That's both a blessing and a curse because if no one else is doing exactly what you're doing but it's so eminently rational—which everyone agrees it is—then their reaction is, 'what am I missing?'

A final statistic. According to BTI, 82% of GC's say that lawsuits are now resolved not on the merits of the case, but based on who can afford to stay in the game, most of which is spent finding the story. This is not justice, not fairness, not "the rule of law." (Let us not, I pray you, lose sight of thos€ values.) It's easy for many of us to talk about improving justice, or access to justice, but imagine if Novus could move that number down by more than 25%, say 50% or more: That would be a contribution to justice with teeth.

$\bullet \bullet \bullet$

Radiant Law

Alex Hamilton, a former Latham & Watkins partner in London, where he co-chaired the firm's global technology transactions group, founded Radiant Law there on January 4, 2011. Entrepreneurs tend to have an itch they need to scratch, and with Alex it was the almost insuperable obstacles the billable hour posed to any serious re-examination of how to deliver legal services in the 21st Century. When one's world, and that of all of one's colleagues, revolves around recording chargeable time, not a moment is left over to rethink things.

So Radiant began with Alex and his colleagues trying to answer the question, "what would a client want in a law firm?" The billable hour would definitely not be on that list, and accordingly Radiant never has and vows it never will keep time sheets—not even internally. Their work is fixed-fee and fixed-fee only.

A logical and obvious place to start the new venture was essentially to permit clients to use Radiant as a platform for outsourcing, or what Alex calls, properly, labor market arbitrage. But since that is intrinsically at risk at better/cheaper entrants in the long run, in the five years since then Radiant has been engaged in a constant process of iteratively discovering what the market actually is willing to engage it to do, and pivoting in those directions.

'his may sound opportunistic and provisional, so I asked Alex what's
nduring and intrinsic. "At the core of Radiant—and a constant from its
1ception—is the triad of 'people, process, and technology.'" Taking them
n reverse order:[73]

- "Technology is always a means to an end," employed only where it
  makes business and commercial sense for Radiant and the client.
  Radiant uses third party products in mature sectors (e.g., document
  creation) but also invests heavily in developing their own proprietary
  software. Perhaps foremost is what Radiant calls its "Remarkable" set
  of add-on tools for Word, which automates many activities lawyers
  normally perform in the traditional Word environment. Among
  other things, Remarkable can rebuild documents that were broken
  up during negotiations, find missing definitions, and check for
  common errors.

- Process means running every engagement through a disciplined
  project management workflow beginning with on-boarding and
  using metrics heavily to track progress against client needs. Learning
  from each engagement is fed back into the process to enhance it
  in future.

- Finally, the "people" component, the only one of these three that
  conventional law claims distinction in, struck me as distinctive at
  Radiant because they emphasize their expertise in IT, technology,
  and business process optimization—not just the lawyers lawyering.
  Indeed, they state unequivocally: "Above all, we understand our
  clients need a contract to deliver their business objectives, not that
  the contract is an objective in itself." In other words, business in the
  driver's seat, law in the back seat.

Almost immediately after its founding, Radiant began moving into
managed services; their first client was the London Stock Exchange.
The market was already moving from outside law firms doing everything,
or almost everything, to a strong turn in the direction of in-house in-
sourcing. Radiant was and is the logical next step, happening in parallel
with the growth in in-house legal capability.

---

73   Quotes drawn from Radiant Law, "About Us," http://www.radiantlaw.com/
about-us/ (October 2016)

Now, the phrase "managed legal services" can seem jargonish, but Radiant has laid out what it means and how it helps address the typical law department's fundamental challenge of being asked to do more with fewer resources and at the same time deliver unquestioned business value. The core components of Radiant's managed services (here using the example of contract management for the client):

- Needs analysis and design. Rather than Radiant assuming, as law firms are wont to do, that they know best what the client needs— or worse, that whatever the lawyers and the law firm are most comfortable doing *must* be what the client needs—Radiant delves into such details as the complexity and type of the contracts, the client's desired service level, and touch points with the business.

- Next, a pilot is often undertaken at the client to test the delivery model and begin to build reporting and tracking dashboards customized to the client's business needs.

- A triage and intake system is then set up with an online portal Radiant provides or using structured forms; it all includes documentation, training videos, and expert system applications to help standardize matters.

- Finally, the system is run using a playbook of pre-agreed clauses, negotiating points, and fall-back positions to ensure consistency and speed time to closing of deals.

- But they're not done: Continuous improvement using reporting against pre-agreed metrics is used to feed back into and refine the system going forward.

All of this may strike you as simply good managerial hygiene, and across most of the business world it would be recognized simply as that. But we all know Law Land is different; I would challenge you to find a conventional law firm operating with systems as rigorous, comprehensive, and transparent as those of Radiant. And there's good reason to expect law firms to continue to operate without their equivalent: Lawyers don't perceive this discipline as valuable—they're all artisans—and the business professionals who might understand its value and have the actual skills to implement it are second class citizens, an inferior caste: "Non-lawyers."

o where is Radiant as a business?

"We're starting to break through from early adopters to the early majority," Alex reported, using *Crossing the Chasm* terminology.[74] We've all seen various ways to conceptually segment legal services according to their risk and frequency—and to infer the optimal source for getting those services performed—but here's Alex's version:[75]

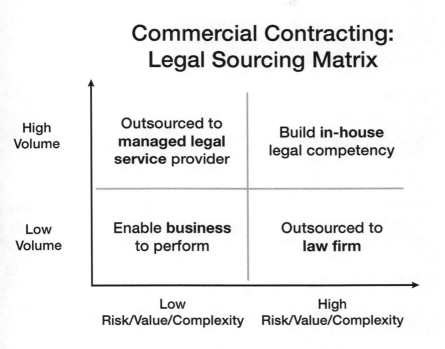

Commercial Contracting: Legal Sourcing Matrix

	Low Risk/Value/Complexity	High Risk/Value/Complexity
High Volume	Outsourced to **managed legal service** provider	Build **in-house** legal competency
Low Volume	Enable **business** to perform	Outsourced to **law firm**

To Radiant, the top left is the most interesting quadrant; the top right and lower left stay within the corporation's four walls, and the lower right still defaults, understandably, to Big Law.

---

74   Geoffrey Moore, *Crossing the Chasm: Marketing and Selling Disruptive Products to Mainstream Customers* (HarperCollins: New York), 1st ed. 1991, 3rd ed. 2014. *Chasm* introduced the concept of the Technology Adoption Lifecycle, which begins with innovators and moves to early adopters, early majority, late majority, and laggards.

75   *A framework for legal sourcing,* June 23, 2016, Radiant Law: http://www.radiantlaw.com/blog/a-framework-for-legal-sourcing/

I ask Alex, as I have every one of the new entrants we're discussing, what types of clients tend to adopt what his firm is offering and where he encounters entrenched resistance.

"We decided law firms were a lost cause," he says with a laugh. "We tried to deal with law firms but there was always one partner somewhere who'd say they prefer not to; basically, law firms talked a lot and never went anywhere. We came to the fundamental realization that it would be most fruitful for us to be working with big companies because offering the kind of managed services we do is a volume play. It makes most sense to clients facing the classic pressure of budgets being cut and headcounts frozen, and who have lots of matters they simply have to deal with.

Within that world, you have to be smart about the type of company you're dealing with. Obviously there's a very wide range of companies that have very different margins: Thinking in terms of the BCG matrix, companies that are mature and in market share battles care a lot about doing things more smartly. Companies on a rocket ride up don't care.

Also, you clearly find very different individuals at each company; General Counsel who are very conservative want everything to be done by Skadden or Latham. Other GC's are more laissez-faire and just want the work to get done, and so are willing to let the team try things differently. This is very hard to see from the outside.

"Are the Big Four accounting firms a genuine threat to Big Law?," I ask.

"Yes, they're very much for real; the reason I'm sure of that is that they keep going out of their way to say they're not going to be a big deal."

"What about machine learning and AI?"

"We don't use expert systems, we use document automation; but it's amazing how much expertise is built into document automation." It's low level, and not being talked about, but every time you add an if-then statement to a document generating system you've replaced a human decision point.

n Alex's own training, he went from being completely at sea to being able
o walk into a room and declare that at the end of the day we're going to
•e negotiating these five points. He believes the same thing is beginning to
appen with expertise embedded in systems.

And the single most salient thing about Radiant?"

When you're working in a world where everything revolves around the
•illable hour, it's a harsh master indeed. Not because you have to 'hit
our numbers,' although that's bad enough; but because it's relentless and
yrannical in its demands. You can never just sit back and think.

upposedly that's why clients hire top-flight lawyers but at least until you're
t the very top of the pyramid it's swimming upstream to spend time re-
lecting hard and trying to be creative for your client. Eliminating billable
lours frees us to do that."

• • •

Riverview Law is UK-based but operates globally and targets as customers
or its Managed Service and Project work the in-house legal departments
of Fortune 500's and FTSE 250's. For its Technology services it targets in-
louse teams globally.

Riverview was founded in 2011 under CEO Karl Chapman. Karl had
een CEO of AdviserPlus, an HR advisory outsourcing business which he
tarted in 1999. AdviserPlus delivered HR and Employee Relations services
o large companies under fixed price, multiyear contracts, both online and
oy phone. As customers came to rely more and more on AdviserPlus and
he benefits of its proprietary technology platform (e.g. process efficiency,
lata and analytics), it perhaps should have come as no surprise that they
began asking for employment-related legal work as well, and the seed of
what became Riverview was planted.

As of late 2016, Riverview has blue-chip clients and annual revenue
approaching £10M, which has been growing at 50% year on year.

Riverview offers three primary products/services; Managed Services,
Projects and Technology.

First, managed services catering to in-house departments who decide it's appropriate to outsource a defined range of activities—say, routine commercial litigation or contract negotiation and compliance.   The objective is to spare the in-house team from being a fire brigade so that the corporation can shift its limited internal legal resources upstream to do more valuable work.

Within this admittedly expansive area, Riverview has found it most productive to focus on the larger corporate in-house teams and the 60-70% of the work that they do day-in, day-out, which can be analyzed, routinized, and packaged into long term contracts.

In a nutshell, Riverview permits in-house departments to free up their resources to move up the corporation's own internal value chain. One could logically expect or hope that higher visibility of the in-house lawyers providing more substantive legal advice, might redound to their benefit in pay, seniority, and trust.

Example: HSBC outsourced its low-complexity procurement work to Riverview three years ago. So far so good, but what happened during just those brief 36 months reveals a more interesting story. The Riverview team of ten or so staffers has since been able to move its own work up from low into midlevel complexity issues. Meanwhile, HSBC internal lawyers are still face to face with the high-level work.

The dynamic that got my attention is that about 25% of the low-level work as of three years ago has simply disappeared, displaced by technology and self-service. What constituted Riverview's "low end" portfolio in 2013 is substantially different in 2016 thanks to the HSBC legal team's collaborative drive for efficiency and quality. This has had two results: As Riverview's managed services have moved up the value curve so has the HSBC internal team, reducing outside counsel spend in the bargain.

Essentially, the Riverview managed services offering constitutes a substitution of cheaper/better/smarter labor. But—critical distinction—unlike our near-shoring/off-shoring law firm operations centers discussed earlier, Riverview's services are enabled by and rest on a proprietary software platform called "Kim" (Knowledge, Intelligence, and Meaning),

hich has become an integral component of Riverview's offerings since its
cquisition of a U.S. Artificial Intelligence business in 2015. Kim, which
; a subsidiary of Riverview, has substantial IP (a classic instance of a
arrier to entry), but interestingly has set up the company as a standalone
echnology business with its own leadership team and a growing list of
ustomers who have contracted directly. "Kim is industry and function-
gnostic, so Legal is just the starting point" explained Kim's Chief
Justomer Officer, Andy Daws.

ringing us to Riverview's second major offering and line of business:
icensing the Kim platform so you can do it yourselves. Riverview has
sed the Kim platform to create "virtual assistants" which can, for example,
erform triage with new matters coming in to the law department to assign
ach case to the right person. The "right" person is a function of various
actors, including the matter's risk profile, which Kim automatically
ssesses based on existing parameters and experience; and a blend of the
ssigned individual's workload and expertise.

he goal is easy to state, difficult to accomplish: To get the work to the
ight people at the right time and with the appropriate level of urgency,
nd to perform it at the right price. None of this can be truly managed
vithout data, so Kim also generates real-time dashboards displaying a
ange of activity and trend data, aimed at the legal department as well as
ts business customers (hence Riverview's slogan, "Legal Input. Business
Jutput."). Beyond data and tracking, Kim contains embedded dynamic
vorkflow and case management, document review and management, and
utomated web services for seamless integration with third-party systems.

n terms of specific product offerings, Kim comes at three price points and
lepths of functionality: "Foundation" is cloud-based, can go live in one
lay, and is preconfigured. "Professional" can be given the look and feel
the "branding") of the client's organization and workflow; and document
emplates, dashboards, and integration with legacy systems (API's) can all
e customized. Finally, "enterprise" makes the Kim technology completely
nvisible to those using it, as it integrates fully into the client's existing
ystems and processes using public, private or hybrid cloud configurations.

As an example of "enterprise," Vodafone is deploying Kim across its global
organization as a clickable icon available to its sales force and customer

service representatives which, depending on the flow of the interaction with the customer, the Vodafone representative can call up to customize an instruction form (prepopulated by Kim with Salesforce and other internal data) or, of course, route more complicated and delicate matters to legal resources, automated or human.

In my conversations with Riverview and Kim, I asked what particular industries or sectors they found most responsive to their offering. Not surprisingly, financial services represents the largest number of clients (a sizable majority in terms of revenue at this time) since that sector tends to spend the most on risk management and compliance, but the model is sector-agnostic and "we have clients ranging from consumer packaged goods to pharma and retail."

Kim has separate technical and back-end capabilities, some of which are useful indeed: For example, enabling knowledge workers to configure a production-ready instance of Kim entirely on their own in a matter of hours, without needing to ask IT for a single line of coding. Whether or not a lawyer or paralegal devotes those few hours to dedicated "teaching" of Kim, Kim is constantly monitoring what attorneys and other data-handling employees actually do and by implication seem to prefer in a workflow, and make recommendations regarding changes to existing processes or risks associated with a particular course of action.

Karl described it this way:

> In this sense Kim works from the inside out, not the outside in, because it enables knowledge workers—operational subject matter experts with no IT development or programming skills—to describe and automate their existing or desired business solutions, processes and workflows.

However impressive, this is less germane to our purposes here today.

I asked Karl how he envisions the future of Riverview, and by extension the legal services industry. He had actually foreshadowed this in a quote contained in a 2014 Harvard Business School Case Study on Riverview:[76]

---

76   *Riverview Law: Applying Business Sense to the Legal Market,* Heidi Gardner and Silvia Hodges Silverstein, June 4, 2014 (Case #9-114-079), © President and Fellows of Harvard College.

One way or another, the big offices, the wood paneling, the massive conference rooms, the armies of young associates slaving away are going to be transformed. Legal in the future will be a whole new game from today because it is finally being subjected to the same pressures that other disciplines have been subjected to for decades.

With me, he was more succinct:

> Kim is a leading indicator of where the market's going; by productizing services, Riverview and other new entrants will disintermediate large swaths of the [legal services] supply chain.

. . .

From the perspective of business model diversity, the world of new entrants could scarcely be more different from that of Law Land. Law firms—in most things that matter, such as career paths, revenue models, and organizational governance—hew essentially to one invariant business model.

New entrants are all over the place.

Some are capital-intensive, some labor-intensive; some have technology at their core, others are trying to build ecosystems of supply and demand. Some employ high ratios of lawyers to business professionals, some the reverse. They're venture funded, angel funded, self-funded, cashflow positive and negative, rocket ships and tractors tilling their fields. Some cater primarily to corporations, others to law firms, and some don't care as long as the clients' checks clear.

Actually, they do have one commonality: If any of them ever tried, they long ago gave up on trying to convince law firms to use what they provide or to partner with them. They go directly to the clients, who will listen thoughtfully and are willing to explore.

More important, I submit, is a subtler but critical difference in modalities of failure. Law firms that fail do so almost universally of self-inflicted wounds: Internal dissension, dereliction in succession planning, battles to the death over ego, and simple exhaustion. But new entrants that have and will fail will almost all fail *because the market passed judgment* and found their offering lacking.

You may think this harsh, but I celebrate it. The market may be impersonal and indifferent, but its vigilance brings with it an essential and bracing discipline. New entrants are continuously trying to figure it all out: To offer something more effective and/or more economical and/or simpler to understand and adopt. Law firms continue to march along to their own drummers. In their intensely internal focus lies true peril. New entrants have and will have innumerable business challenges, but endlessly paying more attention to themselves than to their customers will rarely be one of them.

Disciplined by the market, they will evolve. Quickly.

"When clients require disaggregation, you have to have a response as a law firm: One response is to say we'll abandon the low end work and just do the high end work. That's fine, but that's a shrinking island and there are lots of people trying to get on that island.

"What we're seeing is the industrialization of law; and we're not just seeing it in the law, but in professional services, healthcare, education—everywhere knowledge workers have ruled the roost for the past 50 years."

—David Morley, Senior Partner/Executive Chairman
Allen & Overy (2016

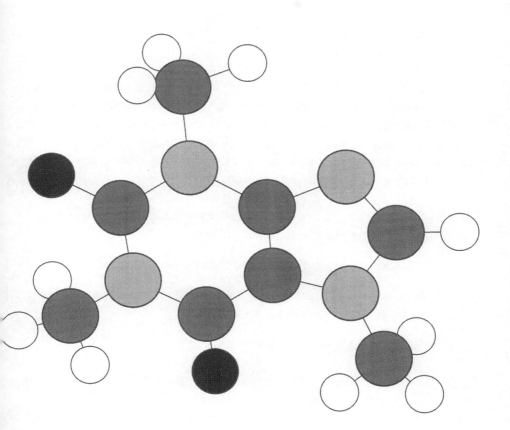

Networks Win

I believe it has long been the case, but now it's accepted wisdom, that clients are increasingly choosy--discriminating and sophisticated--about selecting law firms for each and every individual matter. Sometimes price is no object (this is the "shrinking island" of work that David Morley alludes to) and sometimes, well, good enough is good enough. Which is which? "It depends."

Increasingly, clients, and the very same clients, are pursuing a flight to quality *and* a flight to economy. It's the middle that they're evacuating.

Clients' increasing levels of discernment and pickiness about which law firms get which type of work is now recognized as a commonplace, but less well understood is the parallel phenomenon whereby clients move work, or large pieces of it, not from one law firm to another but from a law firm to a non-law firm--to another organization in the greater universe of legal service providers, of which law firms are only a subset.

This is disaggregation in action. We know from rudimentary economics and business history that disaggregation is:

- Ubiquitous across industries and functions;

- Ever present as a threat even if it seems not to have materialized yet in your corner of the world; and

- For all practical purposes, irreversible.

It's ubiquitous across the economy for the simplest of reasons: It's the flip-side to the "core competence" mantra that has been afoot in Corporate Land for decades at this point, ever since the late, hardly lamented era of high-flying Icaresque conglomerates like Litton, Ling Temco Vought, ITT, Gulf + Western, and Textron. Today, Management 101 insists that your firm stick to its knitting, do what it does best, focus on the core, etc.

-that is to say, become truly expert in one or a handful of indispensably omplementary functions, and try to own that market. [77]

t's an ever present threat because as soon as an industry begins to get arge enough for outsiders to take notice--and Law Land achieved that istinction decades ago--some of them begin to wonder if they couldn't hare in some of the conspicuous wealth being created.

wo drivers of scale operate here, one from the top, as it were, and one rom the bottom. The top I just alluded to: When an industry achieves toticeable size, even a small slice begins to look attractive. The dynamic nabling new entrants to come up even at very small scale--from the bottom--has become vastly more powerful just in the past few years hanks to developments such as cheap cloud computing, widespread and tser-friendly tools for instant collaboration across time and distance, nd, ironically, the rapid disaggregation that has overtaken all the arious industries that grew up around necessary but unsexy corporate nfrastructure such as accounting, payroll, benefits, customer relationship management, inventory control, and of course IT management--all of which are themselves delivered from the cloud.

The minimal efficient size of a firm, in short, is much smaller than it used o be, and shrinking fast.

What does the sudden ubiquity of cloud-sourced services have to do with he "efficient scale" of a firm?

We have known the answer at least since 1937 when the (subsequent) Nobel Prize winner in Economics Ronald Coase published a modest article of barely 14 pages in *Economica* entitled "The Nature of the Firm."[78]

---

77   This, by the way, is why I doubt that in-house law departments will grow to the sky. The dynamic has tended to be one of oscillation, not steady expansion—although as they say past performance is no guarantee of future results. The grow/shrink/grow sine wave looks like this: The CFO and the GC decide cost savings are to be had by hiring in-house lawyers to do what they're renting outside counsel to do, growing the legal department. At some point the GC's budget gets the (usually new) CFO's attention and the department is drastically pruned on the grounds that "having a law firm under our roof is not a core competence."

Repeat.

78   Available today from many sources, including, e.g., http://www3.nccu.edu. w/~jsfeng/CPEC11.pdf

Coase was then all of 27 years old, having been born in a London suburb in 1910, attending the London School of Economics from 1929 through 1932, and studying what was then called "industrial law" (commercial law to us) with the intent of becoming a lawyer. He changed his mind after a year-long tour of the United States on a scholarship to study American industrial structure.[79]

The Nature of the Firm answered a simple question that apparently no one had taken on before: Why do firms exist? Why, that is, aren't we all freelance independent contractors capturing all our value-added to the economy for ourselves?

Coase's answer was that firms make economic sense when they can eliminate the transactions costs of coordinating activity and decision making. After all, classical economics would suggest that if the market is efficient (a bedrock assumption) and that those who are best at providing each good or service are already doing so, it would be optimal to contract out for each individual task. Resources should presumptively be organized by the price mechanism and not organizational management, with all its well-known foibles and pitfalls, including bureaucracy, office politics, agent/principal conflicts, an insular focus, and so on.

Coase's insight was that that's not the end of the story. Contracting outside for each activity involves transaction costs, to be sure, but also searching for and finding the optimal providers, bargaining over price, policing and enforcing performance, safeguarding trade secrets, and so on. Often it's cheaper just to hire people and manage them.

All else equal, firms will be smaller:

- The higher the managerial and administrative overhead costs of the organization itself;

---

79   Coase spent his life in academe, teaching at the Dundee School of Economics and Commerce, the University of Liverpool, the London School of Economics, and after relocating to the United States in 1951, at the University of Buffalo, the University of Virginia, and the University of Chicago (1964—his retirement in 1982). His Nobel award came in 1991.

Coase died, intellectual faculties fully intact, in 2013 at age 102. See *Ronald Coase: 1910 – 2013*, Adam Smith, Esq. (September 3, 2013): http://adamsmithesq.com/2013/09/ronald-coase-1910-2013/?single

- The more likely managers are to make mistakes and the less capable they are of exercising their control over a broad span; and

- The lower the economies of scale in organizing.

Ubiquitous and global online connectivity, 24/7, enable smaller organizations to replicate or exceed the capabilities of larger organizations on almost every measure.[80]

Back to Law Land.

---

[80]   For many 1L's taking Torts, and I'm sure a fair number of their professors and even some practitioners, *The Nature of the Firm* is a metaphorical footnote in Coase's *oeuvre* next to *The Problem of Social Cost,* his 1960 blockbuster, reputedly the most cited law review article of all time, although both articles clock in at over 20,000 citations

Here's how I described *The Problem of Social Cost* in 2013 when I was moved to publish a remembrance of Coase on Adam Smith, Esq. (id.):

His second famous paper took on another bedrock assumption, that the only way to keep people and firms from doing things that injured others (polluting is the classic example) was to impose governmental regulation. Again, he pointed out that that was not necessarily so if transaction costs were sufficiently low—so that the affected parties could negotiate directly and settle the conflict privately. The goal of assigning liability should be to minimize transaction costs, not to assign blame.

The notion that liability should be imposed on the "cheapest cost-avoider," as the shorthand has it, was not just unheard-of but deemed implausible in the extreme.

Using the example of a polluting factory, it's cheaper to assign primary responsibility to the factory not because it's "at fault" but because the alternative, assigning responsibility to the downwind neighbors, would incur insuperable transactions costs as they attempted to organize into a coherent bloc to negotiate with the factory, all the while avoiding the devilish problems of free-riders, holdouts, and so on. But Coase's fundamental insight was that *no matter where liability was assigned the same 'optimal' level of pollution would be negotiated.*

This was so counterintuitive that the famous story is told of Coase having to defend his thesis (here, from the University of Chicago Law School's essay on Coase's passing): Coase described being invited to defend [a previous paper on the FCC's allocation of broadcast spectrum asserting essentially the same thesis] at University of Chicago Professor Aaron Director's home. [The assembled luminaries included Rueben Kessel, Milton Friedman, Martin Bailey, Arnold Harberger, Gregg Lewis, John McGee, Lloyd Mints, and George Stigler.] Coase was able to persuade them to his view that as long as legal rights are properly defined, efficient solutions will prevail. He was asked to write an article for *The Journal of Law and Economics,* which Director had recently founded. The outcome was "The Problem of Social Cost."

"Had it not been for the fact that these economists at the University of Chicago thought that I had made an error in my article on The Federal Communications Commission, it is probable that 'The Problem of Social Cost' would never have been written," Coase said. George Stigler,1982 Nobel Prize winner, later wrote about that night: "We strongly objected to this heresy. Milton Friedman did most of the talking, as usual. He also did much of the thinking, as usual." In the course of two hours of argument, the vote went from 21 against and one for Coase to 21 for Coase.

Here's how one firm, Allen & Overy, represents the new explosion of choices clients have when selecting legal service providers. The players may and surely will change over time, but markets abhor a vacuum and any profitable niche will find occupants.

Stepping back from Law Land:

In his keynote on the opening day of the 2016 Detroit Auto Show, the always outspoken Fiat Chrysler CEO Sergio Marchionne delivered this message (emphasis mine):

> He warned the adoption of electric technology risked continuing the process that he called "disintermediation," under which carmakers have gradually lost control over elements of a vehicle's contents to suppliers.

> "It's been a very steady, rigorous process of disintermediation."

Having initially manufactured all their own components, **carmakers currently retain primary control of making only vehicles' powertrains — their engines and transmissions —** he added.

"If we start losing any of that … we will not be able to hang on to any proprietary knowledge and control of that business," said Mr. Marchionne. "We won't be manufacturing the batteries. We won't be manufacturing the electric motors that are part of that powertrain."[81]

Earlier I made somewhat passing mention of Tesla and Google having a fundamentally different approach to the automotive industry. This is where it comes home to roost.

Here's a vivid illustration of how far disintermediation has gone at the highest end of car land, showing the suppliers of many, but by no means all, of the components of the 2017 Mercedes-Benz E class.[82] If you could see the original at full size, you'd see that among the hundreds of "disintermediated" suppliers are such capable firms as BorgWarner for the turbocharger, Johnson Controls and Magna for much of the instrumentation, Bosch for fuel injection, Thyssen Krupp for suspension components, Honeywell for brake pads, Pirelli for tires, TRW for electroni switches, and so on and so on. I have no doubt they'd be equally willing to sell their expertise and products to Tesla and Google, or Apple for that matter. To call Mr. Marchionne's warning "existential" is no exaggeration.

And it's little more than one step from automakers losing control of the powertrain to law firms losing control of David Morley's "shrinking island

---

81   Financial Times, *"Sergio Marchionne says carmakers risk losing proprietary control,"* January 11, 2016, at https://www.ft.com/content/df1d7bb8-b889-11e5-bf7e-8a339b6f2164. Tellingly, one of the commenters to the article wrote: "It seems to me the auto industry is ripe for transformation and I suspect there is not much they can do about it."

82   Automotive News Europe, http://europe.autonews.com/assets/PDF/CA62017619.PDF

Suppliers to the new Mercedes-Benz E class

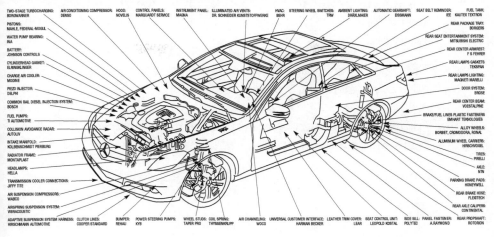

If we step back, or up, one level of generality, what Mercedes, and Apple with its "Designed in California/Manufactured in China" mantra, and Boeing, with its 787 Dreamliner—surely some of the most sophisticated companies in the world—are all doing is orchestrating a networked supply chain.

Let's go into each in a bit more detail.

Apple

Apple, seemingly uncharacteristically for such a secretive place, actually publishes a list of its top 200 suppliers.[83] Some of the key ones are:

- Analog Devices (Norwood, MA) for capacitive touch screen controls using components from Ireland, the Philippines, and the US.

- Jabil Circuit (China) for phone casings and more.

- Micron Technology (Idaho) for DRAM, LPDDR3 and LPDDR4.

- Murata Manufacturing (Japan) for ceramic capacitors.

---

83   As of 2015, https://www.apple.com/supplier-responsibility/pdf/Apple_Supplier_List_2015.pdf

- Qualcomm for cellular baseband modems and GSM/CMA receivers and transceivers.

- Samsung, ironically perhaps (Korea, China, the Philippines, and the US) for flash memory, mobile DRAM, and various application processors.

- STMicroelectronics (Geneva) for low-power three-axis gyroscopes and accelerometers.

Apple's suppliers by country were enumerated and illustrated in a 2014 article,[84] and the breakdown looked like this:

- China: 349

- Japan: 139

- US: 60

- South Korea: 32

- Philippines: 24

- Germany: 13

- Mexico: 7

- Turkey: 6

- France: 5

- UK: 3

- Etc.

Thanks to publicity about fair labor standards and practices, or the lack thereof, the complexity of Apple's supply chain is widely known at least superficially. What relatively few observers know, however, is that when Apple designs hardware it does so almost without regard to how it might be manufactured. Creating a product that is *"insanely great"*—easy to use, intuitive, and beautifully designed—is the first and only priority.

---

84   *How & Where iPhone Is Made,* September 17, 2014, CompareCamp: http://comparecamp.com/how-where-iphone-is-made-comparison-of-apples-manufacturing-process/

nly after that phase is complete does Apple turn its attention to how the component parts might actually be manufactured at mass-market scale nd at mass-market cost. If the right equipment doesn't exist, they'll vent it, either themselves or with their manufacturing partner of choice r the component in question.

ccording to multiple reports, Apple invested $10.5-billion in supply chain bots and machinery in 2013 to assist in building the iPad and iPhone 5.[85]

> "Their designs are so unique that you have to have a very unique manufacturing process to make it," said Muthuraman Ramasamy, an analyst with consulting firm Frost & Sullivan, who has studied the use of the machinery. "Apple has so much cash that they can invest in cutting-edge, world-class machinery that is typically used for aerospace and defense."

his turns the conventional design/engineering relationship on its head. any normal manufacturing company, engineering tells design what's ossible (or design simply assumes it will have to work with the existing aterials and equipment, and never asks engineering to go any further).

> "Most companies will hire a design firm to create a rendering of a product, throw it over the wall to China and then it's the Chinese engineers who do the detailed engineering work," said [Cormac] Eubanks, [product development director at industrial design firm FrogDesign, and] a mechanical engineer. "What Apple does is hard and it takes a lot of time and money."[86]

Vhen you approach the process by assuming you have to operate with vhat everyone else down the street also has, you get a lot of "me too" esults. Not Apple.

---

5   Quoted in Bloomberg, *Apple's $10.5B on Robots to Lasers Shores Up Supply Chain* (November 13, 2013): http://www.bloomberg.com/news/articles/2013-11-13/apple--10-5b-on-robots-to-lasers-shores-up-supply-chain?cmpid=yhoo

6   Id.

Boeing

Boeing assembles its 787 Dreamliners in Everett, Washington and North Charleston, South Carolina, but "assembles" is the operative term. 70% of the plane's parts come from America and 30% from abroad. By country of origin, here are some of the major components:

- Japan (lavatories and interiors, center wing box, main landing gear wheel well and wings and fixed trailing edge of wings),

- Italy (center fuselage and horizontal stabilizers),

- Korea (wingtips),

- Germany (main cabin lighting),

- Canada (wing body fairing)

- UK (landing gear, and engines if they're Rolls Royce),

- Sweden (cargo access doors),

- France (passenger entry doors),

- Australia (movable trailing edge of wings) and of course

- The US (forward fuselage, engine nacelles, aft fuselage, tail fin, and engines if they're GE)

Major suppliers include Rockwell (communications and pilot control), Spirit AeroSystems (fuselage parts), GE or Rolls Royce (engines, of course) [87], and Honeywell (flight control and navigation systems).

---

87   Pratt & Whitney does not supply engines for the 787: *Aeromagazine,* "787 Propulsion System," (3rd quarter 2012: Boeing corporation), at: http://www.boeing.com/commercial/aeromagazine/articles/2012_q3/2/

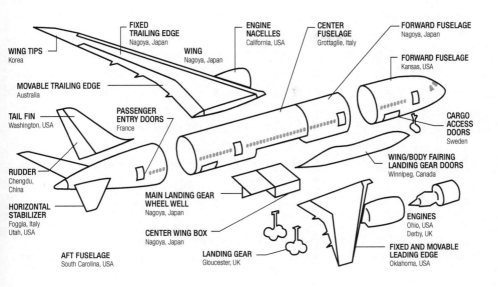

Here's an "exploded" Dreamliner showing the major components by country of origin:[88]

Yes, Boeing experienced birthing pains with Dreamliner assembly at the beginning, mostly because its suppliers weren't finishing components to the extremely fine tolerances Boeing specified so that they would all actually fit together when they mated up in Everett or North Charleston, but tightening down on requirements—and cutting nearly a quarter of the original suppliers—seem to have resolved that.

• • •

Here we've seen three global companies, each of which is leading the way in producing a high-value, fiendishly complex product at the heart of 21st Century life—premium luxury cars, long-haul airliners, and the industry-leading smartphone—who have disaggregated their sources of supply to a fare-thee-well. Clearly they, and their customers, believe specialist suppliers produces a superior product.

Inviting the question: Why should law be different?

88   *The Size of Boeing's Supply Chain,* (Actio, January 19, 2015): http://blog.actio. net/supply-chain-management/the-size-of-boeing-supply/

Because cars, planes, and smartphones are all products and what we provide is a service?

If you were hoping to avoid the compelling logic of picking best of breed when you need, well, best of breed, this feint won't get you there. Or at least the real world economy makes no such irrelevant distinction.

For evidence, I cite you two service industries whose output is every bit as sophisticated, complex, and demanding-to-create as an iPhone or an E Class: Skyscraper construction and full-length feature movies.

Skyscrapers

When a developer receives all the necessary rights and construction funding to proceed with actually constructing an office or residential tower a massive one-off team is assembled to make the building reality: To turn plans and renderings into a form in steel, concrete, and glass.

Using the example of One Vanderbilt Place, a 64-story, 1,514-foot office tower going up adjacent to Grand Central Station in midtown New York as an example, here are the major players:[89]

- Owner/Developer: SL Green

- Architect: Kohn Pedersen Fox Associates

- Façade: Permasteelisa Group

- Main contractor: Tishman Construction

Behind the developer stand banks, insurance companies and pensions funds, and other sources of financing. Behind the architect stand structural engineers and specialists in a host of sub- and sub-sub niches, such as wind load analysis and zoning expediters. Behind the main contractor stand probably the longest roster of all, by number of firms and headcount of individuals involved: Subcontractors for concrete, steel,

---

89   Council on Tall Buildings and Urban Habitat, *The Skyscraper Center*, :   https://www.skyscrapercenter.com/building/one-vanderbilt-place/15833.

The principles discussed vis-à-vis skyscrapers apply at reduced scale to almost any hab itable construction down to single family homes and cottages.

ectrical, plumbing, HVAC, elevators, windows, interior design and build-
ut, and on and on.

nd they're all *service* businesses. Sure, the finished product delivered into
1e market will be one of humanity's more massive creations, but it will be
uilt and assembled by people hired for their talents in particular service
:ctors, and the office building itself will be rented by its future occupants
>r the service the building provides: Space—space with very particular
haracteristics including the most obvious, its location in the center of one
f the leading global metropolises, but also less remarkable but essential
ttributes such as 24/7 accessibility and climate control, ample electrical
apacity/square foot, views, the address's "marquee quotient," and more.

eature films

Iollywood movies, or wide-release feature movies and made-for-broadcast
:ries of any pedigree, have in common with skyscrapers that they're the
roduct of a group of people and organizations with focused, special
ilents coming together in a one-off, never to be repeated configuration to
evelop, produce, and distribute the service called entertainment.

he point is self-evident but consider just the top-line "credits" list for one
f the most famous films of all time, 1997's *Titanic*:[90]

'roduction: Paramount Pictures
)irector: James Cameron
Vriter: James Cameron
'rincipal Cast: Kate Winslet, Leonardo DiCaprio
:ast: Anatoly Sagalevitch, Bernard Hill, Bill Paxton, Billy Zane David
Varner, Frances Fisher, Gloria Stuart, Jonathan Hyde, Kathy Bates, Lewis
.bernathy Nicholas Cascone, Suzy Amis, Victor Garber
)ther cast: ~500 individuals
:xecutive Producer: Rae Sanchini
'roducers: James Cameron, Jon Landau
:o-Producers: Al Giddings, Grant Hill, Sharon Mann
.ssociate Producer: Pamela Easley
√Iusic: James Horner

---

0   IMDB (Internet Movie Database), *Titanic*: http://www.imdb.com/title/tt0120338/
ullcredits/ Functions are listed in IMDB order, which we assume is industry convention.

Cinematography: Russell Carpenter
Editing: Conrad Buff IV, James Cameron, Richard Harris
Casting: Mali Finn
Production Design: Peter Lamont
Art Direction: Martin Laing, Charles Dwight Lee
Set Decoration: Michael Ford
Costume Design: Deborah Lynn Scott

And we also have [approximate headcount]:

- Makeup, >50

- Production Management, 12

- Second Unit Director or Assistant Director, 20

- Art Department, >300

- Sound Department, ~150

- Special Effects, ~50

- Visual Effects, >400

- Stunts, ~125

- Camera and Electrical Department, >300

- Animation, 6

- Casting, 20

- Costume & Wardrobe, 50

- Editorial, 25

- Location, 4

- Music, 40

- Transportation, 25

- "Other crew" (for example: marine consultant, caterer, life guard, naval consultant, accounting estimator, set medic, dive master, dialect coach, craft service, scaffolding engineer, marine rigger, milliner, receptionist, historian, tower crane flagman, filtration technician, animal trainer, housing coordinator, underwater communications, and other trades and vocations you never imagined existed), ~400

More than you ever needed to know about *Titanic*? I might sympathize but I won't.

The point of going into the detail is to enlist your imagination in understanding how complicated assembling such a "network" actually is. Sure, [a writer] + [a director] + [a star or two] = [what we think of as a movie], but under the slick façade it's a Lego assembly of the highest degree of difficulty.

· · ·

What can we learn from this?

We've seen a parade of complex ways to assemble supply chains, which have these features in common:

- The end products and services are at the heart of our 21st Century lives—smartphones, long-haul passenger jets, luxury cars, skyscrapers, feature films;

- They are produced by some of the most complicated supply chains in the world, often put together on a just-in-time basis, with a mutating cast of characters depending on the quite specific requirements of the day and the rising and falling reputations and capabilities of the competitors;

- And one more thing: The firms and teams assembling these networks do so through their own internal cadres of experts who assemble networks for a living.

In other words, for firms like Apple, Boeing, and Mercedes Benz, **assembling, fine-tuning, dissolving, and re-creating networks is and must be a core competence.**

None of those companies could produce what they do were this otherwise.

I submit that the potential implications for Law Land are crystal clear. Consider the parallels.

Legal services: (a) are at the heart of our 21st Century commercial lives; (b) are demanded and supplied globally; and (c) require a host of different capabilities, professions, and vocations to deliver—lawyers, to be sure, but also technology infrastructure, predictive analysis, data security, finance, business process analysis and refinement, marketing (if we ever give it 10% of the due it's accorded everywhere else across the economy), and human resources and professional development.

If "Networks Win," assembling, fine-tuning, dissolving, and re-creating networks that can perform all these functions, just-in-time, will become the core competence in Law Land.

Not the practice of law.

The network architectural gurus will be the scarce talent, at the heart and at the top, of Big Law. You can comfort, and delude, yourself that only lawyers truly understand what legal counsel at the pinnacle of the food chain involves, and that only lawyers can call the shots. Hold tight to that belief and you'll find yourself on the wrong side of what clients believe—and how they're behaving, including on the question of where they're delivering their legal spend. Lawyers will no longer be in the driver's seat. Or, if they do remain there, their firms will slowly erode into competitive irrelevancy as the Masters of the Networks—the General Contractors of Law Land, if you will—decide who's going to do what, when, where, and how. And for what price.

If you disagree, you might ask yourself what your life would look like without smartphones, jets, luxury cars, skyscrapers, and professional cinema—all brought to you by organizations whose core competence is assembling purpose-built one of a kind networks drawing upon external best of breed resources. Then and only then are they capable of delivering a sophisticated, high-value (and seamlessly integrated) product or service.

Apple (flattering myth to the contrary) isn't run by the design department, Boeing isn't subservient to aeronautical engineers, and Mercedes is a

entury past its inventor/tinkerer roots. How much longer can law firms
e run by lawyers?

etwork architects will call the shots.

"When I joined the Bank of England in 1991, I asked the legendary American central banker Paul Volcker for one word of advice. He looked down at me from his great height (a foot taller than I), and said, "Mystique.""

—Mervyn King, The End of Alchemy (2016

Brands Win

All but the most sophisticated clients find it famously difficult to accurately assess the quality of their lawyers. And for even the most sophisticated clients, hiring a Name Brand is often the safest default choice.

But what ingredients create a strong brand? For law firms, the characteristics you'll hear listed are described using words such as quality, prestige, professionalism, judgment, independence, and integrity. Which all boil down, circuitously, to quality.

The firms with the strongest brand names are those deemed to provide the highest quality—and the way you can be assured they're of exceptional quality is because they have the strongest brand names.

Indeed, we have a problem here.

This is scarcely limited to Law Land. Perhaps the most salient, infuriating, and yet utterly understandable reality about reputational rankings is that they're incredibly sticky. Firms (colleges, universities, corporate brands) rank highly because they have sterling reputations which we can confirm by reference to their exalted rank.

As one analyst discussing world university rankings put it:[91]

> "*[Because] rankings are highly stable over time [citations omitted], it is difficult to maintain the fantasy that reputational scores are independent from the rankings themselves. It* would take a massive, discontinuous change in academic quality to notably influence reputation scores in any given year.
>
> Nearly always, the causal chain is that rankings change in response to shifts indicators (e.g., faculty to student ratio), and reputations shift in response to rankings. But clearly, rankings drive reputation not the other way around.
>
> Because reputational assessments are quite susceptible to anchoring effects, and because peer assessments of reputation are strongly correlated with other rankings indicators, reputation scores may

---

91   Araya, Daniel, and Marber, Peter, eds., *Higher Education in the Global Age: Policy, Practice and Promise in Emerging Societies* (Routledge: New York & London: 2014) at 283 (emphasis supplied)

add relatively little value to rankings systems. So what, then, is the purpose of including reputation surveys in rankings formulas? From our perspective, the inclusion of reputation largely serves to maintain the status quo, establishing the credibility of the rankings and ensuring stability in results over time. [...]

Any changes at the top of the hierarchy are bound to gain substantial, largely negative attention. For example, when the California Institute of Technology (CalTech) jumped from number 9 to number 1 in 1999 after *US News & World Report* made a seemingly small change in their overall formula, the substantial public and institutional backlash led *US News* to return to their previous methods in the following year. [...] *Once reputational assessments are formed, they are often quite difficult to change without specific evidence to the contrary.*

Like it or not, university rankings are not a special case. Ten years ago Prof. Bill Henderson made the following observation about the *US News* rankings of law schools:[92]

Academic reputation does not change much over time. Where a school was in 1992 [15 years earlier], which is the first year that U.S. News published its full rankings, explains approximately 93 percent of its current U.S. News academic reputation. Especially for the top 50 schools, there is funnel effect [constricting the universe of possibilities] with progressively smaller variations over time.

Indeed, reputational rankings are so intertwined with pre-existing notions of prestige and quality that they can take on a life of their own utterly divorced from reality and the facts on the ground.

A few years ago Malcolm Gladwell wrote a piece in *The New Yorker*, The Order of Things: What college rankings really tell us,"[93] in which he reported a devilish experiment undertaken in the context of law school rankings. Here it is:

---

2   *Variation in US News Reputation Over Time,* Conglomerate Blog, April 4, 2006: http://www.theconglomerate.org/2006/04/variation_in_us.html

3   February 14 & 21, 2011, at: http://www.newyorker.com/magazine/2011/02/14/ the-order-of-things (emphasis mine)

Some years ago a former chief justice of the Michigan supreme court, Thomas Brennan, sent a questionnaire to a hundred or so of his fellow-lawyers, asking them to rank a list of ten law schools in order of quality. "They included a good sample of the big names. Harvard. Yale. University of Michigan. And some lesser-known schools. John Marshall. Thomas Cooley," Brennan wrote. "As I recall, they ranked Penn State's law school right about in the middle of the pack. Maybe fifth among the ten schools listed. Of course, Penn State doesn't have a law school."

Those lawyers put Penn State in the middle of the pack, even though every fact they thought they knew about Penn State's law school was an illusion, because in their minds Penn State is a middle-of-the-pack brand. (Penn State does have a law school today, by the way.) Sound judgments of educational quality have to be based on specific, hard-to-observe features. But reputational ratings are simply inferences from broad, readily observable features of an institution's identity, such as its history, its prominence in the media, or the elegance of its architecture. They are prejudices.

And where do these kinds of reputational prejudices come from? According to Michael Bastedo, an educational sociologist at the University of Michigan who has published widely on the *U.S. News* methodology, *"rankings drive reputation."* In other words, when *U.S. News* asks a university president to perform the impossible task of assessing the relative merits of dozens of institutions he knows nothing about, he relies on the only source of detailed information at his disposal that assesses the relative merits of dozens of institutions he knows nothing about: *U.S. News. A school like Penn State, then, can do little to improve its position. To go higher than forty-seventh, it needs a better reputation score, and to get a better reputation score it needs to be higher than forty-seventh.* The *U.S. News* ratings are a self-fulfilling prophecy.

Now of course the reputational rankings of Brand Name law firms have not been tabulated, categorized, and published in such monolithic and consistently formatted listing as *U.S. News* college or law school rankings;

ut there are any number of publicly available lists performing similar
unctions, be it the *AmLaw 200,* the UK *Global 100,* Chambers guides,
above the Law, Vault prestige scores, and so forth.

hall we take the Vault guide, which brashly announces it measures
prestige," as our guinea pig to see how much or how little rankings change
over time? Here are the top ten law firms at two different points in time
eparated by a dozen years.[94]

1	Wachtell	Cravath
2	Cravath	Wachtell
3	Sullivan & Cromwell	Skadden
4	Skadden	Sullivan & Cromwell
5	Davis Polk	Davis Polk
6	Simpson Thacher	Simpson Thacher
7	Latham	Latham
8	Cleary	Kirkland
9	Weil Gotshal	Cleary
10	Covington	Gibson Dunn

Care to guess which ranking is as of 2017 and which is from 2006? 2006
on the left, 2017 on the right. But really, is there more than "a dime's worth
of difference?" Enough for you as General Counsel of a Fortune 50 to
ecommend to the Board that they use Cravath in lieu of Wachtell or vice
versa? Cleary before (after?) Latham? S&C before (after?) Skadden? Etc.

'or the record, here are the second 10 for each year:

	2006	2017
11	Kirkland	Weil Gotshal
12	Paul Weiss	Paul Weiss
13	Debevoise	Covington
14	WilmerHale	Sidley

94   Vault Top 100 2007 (showing 2006 rankings) and 2017: at http://www.vault.com/
company-rankings/law/vault-law-100/?sRankID=2&rYear=2007&pg=2 and at http://www.
vault.com/company-rankings/law/vault-law-100/?pg=2

	2006	2017
15	Shearman & Sterling	Quinn Emanuel
16	Sidley	Boies Schiller
17	Williams & Connolly	Debevoise
18	Gibson Dunn	Jones Day
19	Arnold & Porter	Williams & Connolly
20	O'Melveny	White & Case

A bit more movement, to be sure—but remember, these are over a decade apart. And again, putting on your Fortune 50 GC hat, are you really going to point to these rankings when you recommend Weil Gotshal over Debevoise or Jones Day over White & Case? What's impressive is how many of the usual suspects are in materially indistinguishable positions today from where they were over a decade ago.

Probably more than any other profession and to a certainty more than any business, Law Land is a prestige-centric industry. This should come as news to no one but I want to dwell on it for a moment because while we al are aware of the clients' view of which are the "go-to" firms and which are second string, we tend to be focus less on how important it is to lawyers' own self-image.

To individuals who are lawyers, much less partners, at any of the elite firms I've become convinced their status at the firm is a matter of surpassing psychological import and a primary source of self-esteem. Partners at (say) Simpson Thacher or Sullivan & Cromwell don't *work there*; they have internalized that career choice to the point where it's *who they are*. Other firms of the same caliber might serve the same critical purpose, but a lateral move down the prestige ladder—no matter how lucrative and freely willed—would diminish them in not just the eyes of others but their own eyes as well. I think this does more to explain why we so rarely see such moves as all the compensation considerations and angles we see strewn around.

And to those who've ever been at one of these firms, it can serve as a badge of honor for life. Small true story: I was meeting with the managing partner of one of the elite firms recently who noted he had resolved to

ry to attend firm alumni events wherever they happened to be, and he'd
ecently met an older alum effusive about his experience at the firm and
ager to introduce himself to the managing partner. By way of small talk,
ny friend asked the alum when he was at the firm. "For about a year and a
alf, starting in 1979."

Ve can roll the clock back even farther than the decade-ago perspective we
)oked at courtesy of Vault.

Iow about December 1957? A remarkable list was compiled then by one
pencer Klaw in *"The Wall Street Lawyers,"* published in <u>Fortune</u>.[95] My
ource for this found object from history is the invaluable Erwin Smigel's
he Wall Street Lawyer: Professional Organization Man?, published in
964.[96] The "Wall Street firms" are listed in descending order of size by
umber of lawyers, starting with the largest at the time, Shearman &
terling at 125 lawyers, down through #20 Cleary Gottlieb with 46 lawyers:

1. Shearman & Sterling
2. Cravath
3. White & Case
4. Dewey Ballantine
5. Simpson Thacher
6. Davis Polk
7. Milbank Tweed
8. Cahill Gordon
9. Sullivan & Cromwell (tied with Cahill, each at 84 lawyers)
10. Chadbourne Parke
11. Breed, Abbott & Morgan[97]
12. Winthrop Stimson[98]
13. Cadwalader

---

5   Fortune volume 57 (February 1958) at 194.

6   Free Press of Glencoe/Collier Macmillan Limited (New York and London: 1964)
t p. 34 n. 9.

7   The firm where I spent my second year summer and began as the greenest of
ll possible associates—perhaps too civilized and genteel a place to survive, after all.
racing the tree of mergers would take you to today's Winston & Strawn, as would be the
ase for #12, Winthrop Stimson, with which Breed Abbott merged before W&S acquired
ne combined firm.

8   See previous note re Breed Abbott.

14. Willkie Farr
15. Donovan Leisure[99]
16. Lord Day[100]
17. Mudge Rose[101]
18. Kelley Drye
19. Paul Weiss (tied with Kelley Drye, each at 50 lawyers)
20. Cleary

Most of us hadn't even been born when this list was put together, and I wager that no one reading this book today was practicing as a lawyer on Wall Street or anywhere else in 1957, yet what is so remarkable as to border on incredible is how familiar this list is to readers well into the second decade of the 21st Century.

May I hasten to point out that this is distinctly not the case almost anywhere else in the economy. Here's an example:

Interbrand's Best Global Brands[102]

	2006	2016
1	Coca-Cola	Apple
2	Microsoft	Google
3	IBM	Coca-Cola
4	GE	Microsoft
5	Intel	Toyota
6	Nokia	IBM
7	Toyota	Samsung
8	Disney	Amazon
9	McDonald's	Mercedes-Benz
10	Mercedes Benz	GE

99   Disintegrated tragically after aborted merger discussions with Orrick.

100   Lost its way strategically.

101   See: Lord Day, supra.

102   http://interbrand.com/best-brands/best-global-brands/2016/ranking/ and http://www.samsung.co.kr/img/samsung/brand_4.pdf

o be sure, six brands make both lists, but four change. Intel, Nokia, Disney, and McDonald's fall away and Apple, Google, Samsung, and Amazon appear. Perhaps more surprising is where the new 2016 names were in 2006: Samsung was 20th, Google 24th, Apple 39th, and Amazon 5th. Imagine a law firm from the gang of 60—69 as of 2006 vaulting into the top ten a decade later: Inconceivable. (For the record, some of the candidates would have included Heller Ehrman, Holland & Knight, Kaye Scholer, Bingham, and Steptoe & Johnson: Inconceivable doubled.)

Stepping farther back from the world of brands to the world of dominant organizations writ large, here we have the *Fortune 500:*[103]

	2006	2016
1	Exxon Mobil	Walmart
2	Walmart	Exxon Mobil
3	GM	Apple
4	Chevron	Berkshire Hathaway
5	Ford	McKesson
6	ConocoPhillips	UnitedHealth Group
7	GE	CVS Health
8	Citigroup	GM
9	AIG	Ford
10	IBM	AT&T

Even greater turnover, of course, reflecting some of the macroeconomic forces in play during that decade:

- Three petroleum giants on the list in 2006, only one in 2016

- No healthcare companies in 2006, three in 2016

- IBM out, Apple and AT&T in.

All very interesting, you may be saying, all law firms follow substantially the same business model, recruiting from the same talent pool, employing the same revenue model, going after clients drawn essentially from the same pool (businesses and the 1%). Of course you'd expect less turnover at the top of the pecking over time.

And indeed, that's precisely the point, isn't it? Law firm brands are exceptionally sticky, and marketplace perceptions lag reality both on the way up and on the way down. To paraphrase the findings of our cheeky jurist from Michigan, "to get into the inner circle you need to be in the inner circle."

If the elite have been and always will be the elite since time immemorial, world without end—and all the rest of us are just living in their world—it still hasn't gone too badly for everybody else, has it? The vast majority of the AmLaw 200 may not make the shortlist of contenders to deal with potentially catastrophic events, but tens of thousands of people have been making supranormal incomes for their entire careers. So what should we care?

Because of clients.

It's accelerated since the Great Meltdown of 2008, but it was proceeding under the surface before. Clients are moving in two directions at the same time: There's a flight to quality for the most critical matters, and there's a flight to economy for essentially everything else. We've touched on this before in the discussion of "differentiation and speciation," but here it comes back in in the form of very bad news for firms lacking a go-to brand identity.

The flight to economy first: If it's a legal matter that merely has to be dealt with, taken care of, and gotten rid of, good enough is good enough. Even better, and increasingly since the meltdown, economical is the way to go.

[Semantic note: Most people would say "flight to value," not "flight to economy," but I choose to believe that value can be found all the way up and down the food chain at any price point and I think it's worth underscoring the distinction through choice of words. Audi, BMW, and Lexus without question provide quality and value, but few would say hey provide economy. On the other hand, Honda Civic, Toyota Corolla, nd Hyundai Elantra deliver on economy and to many millions of buyers lso provide impressive value, but few would say they deliver a "quality" utomotive experience given the available alternatives.]

ack to why brand matters more than ever: When clients, and their GC's nd Boards of Directors, are facing a hair-raising legal issue, quality is non-egotiable. Brand is non-negotiable. The elite are the only firms who will nake the consideration set; pretenders need not apply.

Conversely, we all know economy when we see it. It's firms with kinder nd gentler rates, yes, but that's a wasting and perishable advantage. The future doesn't belong to those who can arbitrarily cut their rates, ut to firms who invest in developing and continually improving truly ophisticated business process optimization protocols and technology, and naking it an habitual discipline to force work down to the lowest-cost-nost-appropriate staffing, including maximal use of business professionals. Not all firms are capable of this, or willing to make all the tough internal alls it takes to actually do it.

This leaves, mostly, the rest of us.

We who can't/won't/don't know how to go through the serious business process optimization rigor the "economy" route requires, and who aren't in he elite because we're not in the elite.

We're at risk of losing out to the leaders in quality and to the leaders in conomy. We have brands that may not stand for much of anything in particular—even, when administered truth serum, to the leaders of these irms themselves. That's not promising. Brands matter more than ever.

"The fanatic is always concealing
a secret doubt."

—George Smiley, in John LeCarre':
Tinker, Tailor, Soldier, Spy (1975

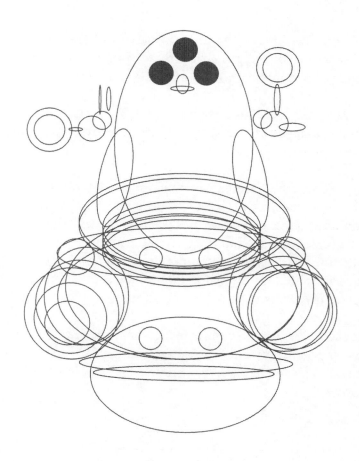

Machines Win

No topic in Law Land strikes me as more polarizing than the future impact of technology. In one camp are true believers positing that we'll all be disaggregated and commoditized right out of a living before we know what hit us. The most prominent proponent of this camp by far in Law Land is my friend Richard Susskind.[104] In the other are equally stalwart deniers celebrating the eternal reign of ineffable and peerless human judgment.

This makes conversations of genuine substance and open-minded inquiry touchy to carry out. You might expect that I subscribe to neither school of thought, and you would be right.

So in discussing this scenario I will attempt to proceed from a practical and grounded perspective, focusing on what objectively does, and might plausibly soon, work.[105]

One more introductory observation which seems left out of the public discourse on machines, technology, and artificial intelligence in terms of their impact on jobs: Will machines destroy jobs like the proverbial neutron bombs, leaving the buildings but eliminating the people, or will the outcome be to create even more new, and better, jobs than those destroyed, as with the famous historical precedent of laborers moving *en masse* from family farms to factories and shops?

This debate, too, seems to be conducted in the form of serial monologues, not genuine engagement. The "robots are coming for you" crowd and the "progress has always led to better and never fewer jobs" crowd talk at cross-purposes.

---

104   *The Future of the Professions: How technology will transform the work of experts* (with Daniel Susskind, Oxford University Press: 2015); *Tomorrow's Lawyers: An introduction to your future* (Oxford University Press: 2013); *The End of Lawyers? Rethinking the nature of legal services* (Oxford University Press: 2008); *Transforming the Law: Essays on technology, justice, and the legal marketplace* (Oxford University Press: 2000); *The Future of Law: Facing the challenges of information technology* (Oxford University Press: 1996); *Essays on Law and Artificial Intelligence* (Tano: 1993); *Expert Systems in Law* (Oxford University Press: 1987).

105   To avoid the risk of being too technical, as well as in hopes of avoiding irrelevant distractions and quibbles, and for the sake of concision, I will use "AI" to embrace the combination of technologies at issue here, including deep and machine learning, pattern matching, recursive and Bayesian analysis, neural networks, facial and visual and voice recognition, and so on.

m not going to predict who's right—I warned you this isn't a book about
redictions—but I'd like to inject an idea into this debate that is grounded
1 basic economic theory and not in the cold sweaty fear of robots taking
ver nor in the potentially inapt parallels to earlier episodes in history.

1troductory undergraduate level economics tells us that when some
nportant activity becomes significantly cheaper—like categorizing data
nd predicting, as AI does—people will use more of it in general and may
ven begin to use it to address problems where it was thought irrelevant or
nhelpful before.

. secondary elementary economic effect is that activities and functions
1at complement the suddenly-cheaper activity become more valuable
nd will be demanded in greater quantity across wider areas of economic
ctivity. If Eli Whitney's invention of the cotton gin revolutionized the
fficiency of spinning cotton into cloth—which it surely did, in 1793—
1en demand for all sorts of activities and products which complemented
otton fabric also spiked: Dyes, industrial textile mills and millworkers, etc.

o the question is what "complements" data categorization and prediction?

venture the complement that matters for our purposes is judgment. If
BM Watson (say) predicts that you or your sister or son are at X% greater
isk for a particular disease, the next thing you're going to want to know
; what to do about it now. The answer to that requires judgment, and at
:ast in the shorter term—perhaps a long enough term to encompass an
ntire career—human beings are in the best position to form and deliver
1at judgment.

.gain, I'm not predicting this straightforward Econ 101 observation
1eans lawyers' jobs aren't at risk from the march of the machines. On the
normous topic of whether the number of jobs destroyed will outnumber
hose newly created, or vice versa, I have no view. I firmly believe, however,
hat the makeup and mixture of jobs in the legal services sector will look
ramatically different than it does today. Finally, I believe it's important
o introduce a hitherto widely ignored perspective grounded in basic
conomic theory on the faith-based rhetorical debate about the machines'
mpact on jobs.

In 1936 the tragic genius Alan Turing introduced his still profound concept of a universal computing machine. Alternatively, more technical writers sometimes call it "the von Neumann architecture," after John van Neumann's 1946 publication of a paper describing what's fundamentally the same concept.[106] Either way, what both terms refer to is a machine that can solve any problem capable of being solved by a computer, or, expressed differently, that any algorithm that can be expressed can be executed or simulated by such a machine.

This may sound subtle or arcane or both, but It provides the basis for everything we think of today as a computer, from Amazon's or Google's massive cloud capabilities to our laptops to the smartphones in our pockets and purses. It was a deep insight: Machines didn't need to be purpose-built for particular one-off functions. Conceived at a high level of abstraction, their possibilities remained open-ended, limited only by human imagination.

I lay out this brief history because I believe something analogous, and equally if not more profound, may be dawning upon us: Artificial intelligence. The analogy is this: If machine learning/AI live up to their promise, we may find they can emulate many of the things human brains can do in the areas of research and analysis (at the very least).

You may deem this an extravagant and far-fetched supposition, but I'm hardly the first to advance it, and I'd like to provide a bit of context around

---

106   Alan Turing (1912—1954) was a ground-breaking English mathematician and computer scientist most famous today for his WWII leadership of the group that cracked the German's "Enigma" code machine at Bletchley Park, which among other things enabled the Allies to defeat the Germans in the Battle of the Atlantic, and has been estimated to have shortened WWII by as much as four years and spared 14 million lives. I called him "tragic" because he was prosecuted for homosexuality in 1952, underwent chemical castration, and committed suicide in 1954 at age 41.

John von Neumann (1903—1957) was a Hungarian-born mathematician and computer scientist, among many other things, who worked on the Manhattan Project under Robert Oppenheimer and focused on one of the earliest mechanical computers of the 20th century, the EDVAC.

Experts could argue that the "von Neumann architecture" is not as expansive as a "universal computing machine," but we don't need to go there.

ow *systemic* technological advances have tended to develop historically
efore going any further down the AI road.

opened this section with the principle of the Turing machine because it
rovides perhaps the first template in the shortish history of computing
r what open-ended platforms can evolve into. The first functioning
al-world Turing machine ("Turing complete," in the lingo) was Colossus,
eveloped improbably enough by the British Post Office Research Station,
t the inspiration of the famous cyber geniuses at Bletchley Park. Used
arting in February 1944 to break Nazi codes, Colossus was programmed
y switches and plugs and not a stored program.[107]

etter known to history was the US Army-funded ENIAC (Electronic
umerical Integrator And Computer), which formally went live on
ebruary 15, 1946 at the University of Pennsylvania in Philadelphia; it
as originally designed to calculate artillery trajectories. It cost nearly
7-million in 2016 dollars to build ENIAC, and by the time it was
ecommissioned in 1955 it consisted of nearly 18,000 vacuum tubes and
ver 5-million hand-soldered connections occupying 1,800 square feet, the
ze of a single-family house. Geeks with too much time on their hands
ave estimated that to duplicate the functionality of an iPhone 6 would
equire about 10-million ENIACs, which would take up substantially more
quare mileage than the City of Los Angeles.[108]

evertheless, both ENIAC and the iPhone 6 are Turing machines, a
undamental technology platform.

robably the most powerful systemic technology platform we use today,
nd certainly the most ubiquitous, is the Internet itself. At a not terribly
igh level of abstraction, the internet is an open-ended platform inviting

---

07   *Colossus Computer,* Wikipedia (undated), at: https://en.wikipedia.org/wiki/
olossus_computer

08   *How big would an iPhone 6 be if implemented using ENIAC technology,* Reddit,
une 29, 2015: https://www.reddit.com/r/estimation/comments/3benfs/how_big_would_
n_iphone_6_be_if_implemented_using/

he economist in me can't resist noting that an iPhone 6 retailed when released for
bout $700, and in today's dollars 10-million ENIAC's would cost about $7-million x
0-million, or $70 x 10^{12} power, which calculates to $70-trillion, nearly four years'
orth of US GDP.

us to do whatever can imagine and wish to do with it: We can connect the Library of Congress or the archives of every published statute, regulation, and case in the United States, and we can also connect our home thermostat or wall oven. We can use it to create Airbnb, Facebook, and Apple iTunes, and also for jihadist recruiting propaganda: The point i that as a systemic platform and the operating system of the online world, it invites us to use it in ways limited only by our imaginations and appetit for capital and labor investment.

This brings us back to AI: It may be the third systemic platform to evolve out of this hardware and software driven substrate. If so, I wouldn't bet o its having too many intrinsic limitations in the long run. Note that when say "intrinsic" limitations, I mean it in a fairly profound sense, as in limits imposed by the laws of physics. Like trying to emulate an iPhone 6 with 10-million ENIAC's: Physical constraints on the speed of electrons throug circuitry [about 40—70% of the speed of light] would mean the clock speed couldn't come anywhere near that of the iPhone and thus it wouldn be able to actually run the Apple iOS fast enough to function.

But as an operating assumption based on decades of humanity's track record with hardware and software, and millennia of our experience with capital and labor investments, I believe the most reasonable forecast vis-à-vis practical obstacles is that they will all ultimately yield.

Similarly, as an operating premise and not a heroic extrapolation, I believe it's premature to "foresee AI threatening to bring about the end of professional practice," as Kingsley Martin recently posed the question.[109] Perhaps the most authoritative and deeply researched article on this topic recently is McKinsey's *Where Machines Could Replace Humans—and whe*

---

109   Kingsley Martin founded KMStandards and has developed software capable of automatically analyzing legal agreements and creating contract standards. He has more than 30 years of experience in law practice and software design and development. Quote from *Artificial Intelligence: How will it affect legal practice – and when?*, Thomson Reuters Forum, Vol 2: Edition 1, 2016.

iey can't (yet) (July 2016),[110] which—bottom line—estimated that 23% f the time spent by lawyers could be automated using proven technology vailable today. While this is not apocalyptic news for lawyers, isn't the 10st revealing aspect of this that we're even having a debate about the iture impact of AI on our daily work?

 few other practical constraints on the speed with which technology—not 1st AI but also mechanical robotic functions—tends to invade any given 1b function. All else equal, substituting machines for human labor is a inction of:

1. Technology's sheer ability or lack thereof to perform the function at an acceptable level—the one and only factor we seem to have in mind when we think about this topic.
2. The costs of automation (always).
3. The costs and scarcity of human workers who would perform the function otherwise.
4. Benefits of automation beyond simple labor cost substitution (e.g., superior quality, reliability, speed, transparency, tractability to continuous improvement, etc.).
5. And social or regulatory constraints or taboos.

Ve've already discussed the first element—not there yet but advancing 1exorably, and technology has Moore's Law on its side.

---

10   http://www.mckinsey.com/business-functions/digital-mckinsey/our-insights/ /here-machines-could-replace-humans-and-where-they-cant-yet

lere's their high-level summary of their findings:

> These conclusions rest on our detailed analysis of 2,000-plus work activities for more than 800 occupations. Using data from the US Bureau of Labor Statistics and O*Net, we've quantified both the amount of time spent on these activities across the economy of the United States and the technical feasibility of automating each of them. The full results, forthcoming in early 2017, will include several other countries,[1] but we released some initial findings late last year and are following up now with additional interim results.
>
> Last year, we showed that currently demonstrated technologies could automate 45 percent of the activities people are paid to perform and that about 60 percent of all occupations could see 30 percent or more of their constituent activities automated, again with technologies available today.

The second, for some mysterious reason, we tend to overlook, but referrin again to the track record of hardware and software it would be bizarre bordering on perverse to believe the future trajectory of cost will be anything other than lower and lower over time.

The third is worth elaborating upon when it comes to Law Land: McDonald's hasn't yet automated burger-flipping, although supremely reliable technology exists to perform that very task, because, well, burger flipping humans aren't very expensive on an hourly basis. This is merely a restatement of, and application of, the essential truth in labor markets that wages are not actually the primary driver of "the cost of labor" when comes to the product or service that's finally delivered: The primary drive: is labor productivity, so a highly expensive but highly productive worker can be a bargain compared to a cheap and unskilled substitute. One also imagines that with the McDonald's example, since the rapidity of burger flipping is driven by cooking time and not the flipper's dexterity, robots wouldn't make an appreciable difference. But this doesn't undercut the point that purpose-built burger-flipping machines are probably a costly and uneconomic substitute for a minimum wage worker who can also be doing other things between flips.

Lawyers, by contrast, are very expensive labor indeed, typically ranked in the top three occupations in annual income by the Bureau of Labor Statistics, and we're not noted for celebrating quantum leaps in our own productivity, so point number three is pointed for us indeed.

Point four doesn't provide us much more solace. Software tools for e-discovery exceeded the accuracy and consistency of lawyers' years ago and the performance of predictive coding and other state of the art tools only keeps improving. So too with document automation, and as for basi "research" technology supplanted manual labor long enough ago that we don't even consider how we find sources "technology" at all; it's just search on a screen instead of through the library stacks on foot—good heavens, how else would you do it?

The fifth point, regulatory or social taboos, presents a mixed picture.

lthough there's little evidence yet of regulatory clampdowns on AI in
w, the drumbeat of alarm can already be detected.[111] Arguments will
e presented that AI-in-law can't be trusted until the day it achieves utter
erfection, much as driverless car technology can't be trusted because
ccidents have occurred.

Vhat these assertions lack is context: AI may err in both situations, but
hat's its batting average or competency rating compared to the human
lternative? That's the only question that should matter to clients (or
rivers and passengers). Whether it's how lawyers and car manufacturers
r the plaintiffs' bar tend to view it is a separate question which, I humbly
ubmit, should carry approximately zero weight. Still, we should probably
esign ourselves to rear-guard actions.

ocial taboos? Hard to imagine. Most ordinary consumers, not to
nention corporate clients, care far more about tangible results than how
ie sausage was made. Consider this recent report and put yourself in the
ioes of a patient arriving at your dermatologist's office with a worrisome
lemish on your skin:

> Skin cancer is the most common of human cancers with about
> one million people diagnosed each year in the US alone. The
> first two types, basal cell and squamous cell, should be treated
> early to avert potential disfigurement if left unchecked but they
> don't tend to spread elsewhere in the body. The third type,
> malignant melanoma, while constituting a small proportion
> overall, is highly aggressive and can be fatal if not treated promptly.
> All skin cancers start as precancerous lesions which are visible to
> the naked eye, which makes inspection and accurate identification
> as to type critical.
>
> The most experienced human dermatologists have about a 75%
> accuracy rate in identifying early-stage malignant melanomas;
> IBM Watson is already at about 95% accuracy tested against the
> same criteria.[112]

---

11   For example, Wendy Chang, *Time to regulate AI in the legal profession?*
Perspective), Bloomberg Business of Law, July 2016: https://bol.bna.com/time-to-
gulate-ai-in-the-legal-profession-perspective/

12   Author's condensation of a segment of a video documentary on Watson
resented by The National Geographic, summer 2016.

Less a matter of life and death than detecting malignant melanomas, but closer to the day to day labor performed by lawyers, was *The New York Times'* report that it has begun to deploy Google "Jigsaw," a natural language processing and interpretation engine, to moderate readers' comments submitted to its online stories. Heretofore comment moderation relied strictly on human editors.

At the *Times*, comment moderation is much more nuanced than, say, removing objectionable words; they evaluate and approve or reject comments depending on subjective judgments of whether a submission, no matter how distasteful, has a basis for the position it's advancing.

So "marriage is between a man and a woman" would be rejected, but "Scripture instructs that marriage should be between a man and a woman" would be approved. "Bitch," no; "you go, bitches!" OK. These distinctions require more than parsing literal meanings.

The background:[113]

> Comments on Times stories are moderated by a team of 14 people known as the community desk. Together, they review around 11,000 comments each day for the approximately 10 percent of Times articles that are open to reader comment.

> The Google subsidiary Jigsaw has developed a tool called Conversation AI, which uses machine learning to identify harassment. Jigsaw trained the tool with the help of institutions, including The New York Times, which provided 17 million reader comments from The Times's website along with decisions that moderators had made about whether to accept or reject them. Analyzing comments that moderators had flagged as abusive helped Conversation AI improve.

---

113   See The New York Times, *Can Bots Fight Bullying*, 21 September 2016, and Insider: *Approve or Reject These 5 Comments*, 20 September 2016: http://takingnote. blogs.nytimes.com/2016/09/21/can-bots-fight-bullying/ and http://www.nytimes.com/ interactive/2016/09/20/insider/approve-or-reject-moderation-quiz.html

1 the near future, the *Times* plans to release the tool as open source for ther online publications to adopt and enhance, and expects to have all of s stories open to commentary, using Jigsaw, in the near future.

1eanwhile, Google makes no secret of its ambitions:

> "We are in the process of transforming into a machine-learning company," Jeff Dean, who is in charge of Google Brain, the company's artificial intelligence project, told me this year. For each problem Google solves this way, it gets better at solving other problems. "**It's a boulder going downhill gathering more momentum as it goes**," Mr. Dean said.[114]

'his neatly brings us to the Big Leagues in terms AI.

very major tech company is pursuing AI as a top priority and all have arly-stage products on the market already: Amazon/Alexa; Apple/ iri; Facebook/FAIR; Google/Google Assistant, DeepMind, and more; BM/Watson; and Microsoft/Cortana-Bing. The CEO of each of these ompanies is on record as saying AI represents their firm's future. according to a cross-section of these firms, voice searches on smartphones nd other devices have gone from "a statistical zero" in 2015 to 25-40% of ueries in late 2016.[115]

Jnderstanding and responding appropriately to a spoken search query is .othing other than AI in action. It requires an understanding of several .imensions of the life of the individual asking the question:

- Context ("How do I get there?" means one thing when you're driving and another sitting at your desk)

- Past behavior (should a search for flights rank the airline where the person is a medallion level flier higher?)

---

14   Farhad Manjoo, *State of the Art: A High-Stakes Bet: Turning Google ıssistant into a 'Star Trek' Computer,* The New York Times, 29 September 2016 ımphasis mine): http://www.nytimes.com/2016/09/29/technology/google-assistant. tml?ref=business&_r=0

15   Innumerable sources of public record.

- Pending plans ("weather in Austin" probably means right now unles the person has a trip there scheduled for next week, in which case it probably means next week)

- Preferences (walk, drive, or subway?)

- Friends and family ("when is Mary's birthday"requires knowing which Mary);

- And the urgency of the query.

Yet we're now using these tools every day with hardly a thought; people as their Amazon Echo's for the sports headlines or to "put on that 80's playlis in the den," and it just works.

This exposes the truth at the heart of the AI researchers' old joke: "As soon as it works, it's not AI: it's just software."

We can see the results already appearing, perhaps most strikingly in DeepMind's "AlphaGo" implementation of AI, which beat the world's mos highly ranked Go player, the 33-year-old Lee Sedol of Korea, in a best-of-five game match held in Seoul in early 2016. Twenty years ago IBM's DeepBlue beat Gary Kasparov, then the world's #1 chess grandmaster, in a six-game match, but Go and chess are utterly different games and that's why AlphaGo's victory marks the progress of machine intelligence into another dimension entirely.

Compared to Go, chess is a rules-driven game played on a relatively limited board with relatively limited options for each player's move at any given moment in a game. This enabled DeepBlue to beat Kasparov by fundamentally by employing brute force computing power without any pretense of instinct or irrational intuitive brilliance.[116] Conceptually, Go exists in another planetary orbit. Because it's unfamiliar to most Western readers, here's a quick introduction:

> At its core, the game of Go, which originated in China more than 2,500 years ago, is an abstract war simulation. Players start with a completely blank board and place black and white stones, one at a time, to surround territory. Once placed, stones do not move,

---

116   *Deep Blue versus Garry Kasparov,* Wikipedia: https://en.wikipedia.org/wiki/Deep_Blue_versus_Garry_Kasparov

and they're removed only if they're "killed"—that is, surrounded completely by the opponent's stones. And so the game goes—black stone, white stone, black stone, white stone—until the board is covered in an intricate tapestry of black and white.

The rules of Go are simple and take only a few minutes to learn, but the possibilities are seemingly endless. The number of potential legal board positions [is] greater than the number of atoms in the universe. Because there are so many directions any given game can move in, Go is a notoriously difficult game for computers to play. It has often been called the "Holy Grail" of artificial intelligence.[117]

hat's why, if DeepBlue's triumph over Kasparov 20 years ago or Watson's ver "Jeopardy" all-stars five years ago are seen as landmarks, AlphaGo's ill come to rank in the same firmament.

√hat makes Go ontologically different from chess is that it has almost o rules. Playing it at a high level is all about experience, vision, and ısight, and not with mechanisms or decision trees or if-then statements.

17   Christopher Moyer, *How Google's AlphaGo Beat a World Go Champion*, 28 larch 2016, The Atlantic: http://www.theatlantic.com/technology/archive/2016/03/the-visible-opponent/475611/

AlphaGo's breakthrough was its demonstration that AI has crossed into decisively new territory.[118]

Let's go back to the "boulder rolling downhill" metaphor: Here's what it means in the real world of human beings and AI, where AlphaGo had lost five-game match to a slightly lower-ranked master just five months before the Sedol match:

> [AlphaGo] is always improving, playing itself millions of times, incrementally revising its algorithms based on which sequences of play result in a higher win percentage. As you are reading this,

---

118   Let us not underestimate the emotional and (forgive me) human impact this has on those who experience it. Here's coverage of Lee's reaction as he was losing the first three of the best-of-five series:

> In Game 2, Lee exhibits a different style, attempting to play more cautiously. He waits for any opening he can exploit, but AlphaGo continues to surprise. At move 37, AlphaGo plays an unexpected move, what's called a "shoulder hit" on the upper right side of the board. This move in this position is unseen in professional games, but its cleverness is immediately apparent. Fan Hui [the lower-ranked opponent AlphaGo beat five months earlier] would later say, "I've never seen a human play this move. So beautiful."

> And Lee? He gets up and *walks out of the room.* For a moment it's unclear what's happening, but then he re-enters the game room, newly composed, sits down, and plays his response. What follows is a much closer game than Game 1, but the outcome remains the same. Lee Sedol resigns after 211 moves. That night, Lee and a group of his colleagues stay up until 6:00 a.m. brainstorming possible strategies. They look for a silver bullet, an Achilles heel, any way to secure a win. He'll now need three wins in a row to win the series.

> * * *

> Game 3 ends in another loss—after four hours of grueling play, Sedol resigns. He's playing some of the finest Go of his career, but he simply can't chip away at the AI's armor. It's clear that AlphaGo's strength surpasses even what was on display in Games 1 and 2. Later, David Ormerod, an American commentator, will write that watching AlphaGo's Game 3 win made him feel "physically unwell." In the end, finding no moves that improve its chances of winning, it begins playing nonsense moves.

> At the post-game conference, Lee looks 10 years older. Amidst a barrage of camera flash bulbs he apologizes to the entire world at once. "I apologize for being unable to satisfy a lot of people's expectations," he says. "I kind of felt powerless." Even the DeepMind researchers, who have a deep admiration for Lee, seem more somber than jubilant at their own victory. There is a sense that something has changed.

Id.

AlphaGo is improving. It does not take breaks. It does not have days when it just doesn't feel like practicing, days when it can't kick its electronic brain into focus. Day in and day out, AlphaGo has been rocketing towards superiority, and the results are staggering.[119]

his is not celebratory boasting: It's part of the intrinsic power of 1achines vs. humans. Machines not only don't get tired or discouraged r distracted, they never forget; they never make exactly the same mistake vice; and they continuously keep getting more capable, faster, smaller, and 1eaper. The implementation of Watson that won Jeopardy in 2011 was 1e size of a master bedroom. The same capability can now fit into a space 1e size of the vegetable drawer in your double-door refrigerator. It's also 40% faster.

recapitulated the history of the Turing machine from ENIAC to the 'hone in some detail for a reason: This is the progress technology can 1ake in our era over the span of a shortish human lifetime. AI is the idustry's focus now. You are at liberty to project for yourself where this 1ight lead.

ut let's not get ahead of ourselves.

1ost people have been skeptical of AI for a very long time. This is nderstandable: The most reasonable attitude based on evidence of its rogress has been something like "sounds magic but I'll believe it when I e it:" The poster child of the technology of an ever-receding tomorrow.

. quite radically separate school of thought has been celebrating the romise of technology for a long time in many contexts. Rather than hoosing sides in this somewhat abstracted and ideologically freighted ebate, let's assess how AI has, and has not, developed so far.

'he essential obstacle to an AI that "works" in the most practical and ommon sense meaning is that AI is not one technology but a combination f tools, algorithms, hardware and software implementations, and datasets f massive scale. AI has been slow to appear real because it requires rogress on so many fronts at once, many of which (cloud processing and ata storage resources, for example) have only existed recently.

---

19   Id.

Because it has required cumulative progress on many seriously hard problems, it has been blocked by what might be called the cursed downside of network effects: Networks without scale have trivial value, and anything that forestalls scale forestalls the network's promise: You can't have anything until you can have everything.

Here's a sort of family tree of AI, representing all the elements required to work at a certain minimum degree of maturity and power before AI can coalesce and become real:

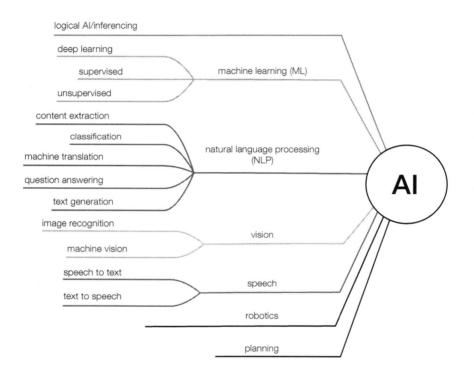

We now appear to be crossing over into having everything.

If you can't have anything until you have everything, the converse is also true. Once networks do achieve a certain critical mass, they can behave like that boulder rolling downhill.

Of course, it does a disservice to AI to lump it in with other network effects we're familiar with, which we primarily experience in terms of lock-in,

r better or worse: Facebook is where you go because call your friends
o there, Ebay is where all the buyers and sellers are, and Google the best
earch engine because it's where almost everyone searches.

ut AI is not at all a network comparable to these: It's a systemic platform,
ke the Turing machine or the net itself.

onceiving of AI this way forces one to look at postulated limits on its
otential reach with at least skepticism, if not a presumption that they may
ell prove to be rather parochial fallacies sooner or later. Predictive coding
ill never surpass the quality and reliability of associates? Machines can't
atch highly trained professionals diagnosing life-threatening conditions
ke melanoma? They can beat grandmasters at chess with rules and brute
orce but not the world's best Go player through deep learning?

oogle calls its suite of AI research and products "Google Brain," with the
elf-proclaimed and not noticeably humble mission to "Make machines
ntelligent. Improve people's lives."

[ere's how they describe one of the primary components, computer
ystems for machine learning:[120]

> Key to the success of deep learning in the past few years is that we
> finally reached a point where we had interesting real-world datasets
> and enough computational resources to actually train large,
> powerful models on these datasets. The needs of new applications,
> such as training and inference for deep neural network models,
> often require interesting innovations in computer systems, at
> many levels of the stack. At the same time, the appearance of new,
> powerful hardware platforms is a great stimulus and enabler for
> computer systems research.
>
> One key way to accelerate machine learning research is to have
> rapid turnaround time on machine learning experiments, and we
> have strived to build systems that enable this. Our group has built
> multiple generations of machine learning software platforms to

---

20   *Research at Google* (undated), at: http://research.google.com/teams/brain/
omputer-systems/. See generally: *Google Brain Team,* at http://research.google.com/
eams/brain/

enable research and production uses of our research, with a focus on the following characteristics:

- **Flexibility**: it should be easy to express state-of-the-art machine learning models, such as the ones that our colleagues are developing (e.g. RNNs, attention-based models, Neural Turing Machines, reinforcement learning models, etc.).

- **Scalability**: turnaround time for research experiments on real-world large-scale datasets should be measured in hours not weeks

- **Portability**: models expressed in the system should run on phones, desktops, and datacenters, using GPUs, CPUs, and even custom accelerator hardware

- **Production readiness**: it should be easy to move new research from idea to experiment to production

- **Reproducibility**: it should be easy to share and reproduce research results

Things are moving fast and Google makes no secret that it's "ambitious." Google's first system, released in 2012, performed well on three of those five criteria, but its newest system excels on all of them.

But seriously, how different is AI from very good plain old software? We've recently seen a dramatic example.

Google Translate was introduced in 2006 and has become among the company's most popular and useful products. It's now integrated into Gmail, Chrome, and other Google products, as well as existing independently as a stand-alone app—very good plain old software. Late in 2016 the Google Brain team clicked a virtual switch and converted Translate to an AI-based system. Building the "AI Translate" product from start to finish took a mere nine months, which is virtually overnight on software development calendars. Here's how the old and the new systems did with a Jorge Luis Borges quote, *"Uno no es lo que es por lo que escribe, sino por lo que ha leido."*[121]

---

121   As recounted in *The Great A.I. Awakening,* The New York Times Magazine (Dec 14, 2016), at: http://www.nytimes.com/2016/12/14/magazine/the-great-ai-awakening.htm l?action=click&pgtype=Homepage&region=CColumn&module=MostEmailed&version=Fu l&src=me&WT.nav=MostEmailed&_r=0

Old (software)	New (AI)
"One is not what is for what he writes, but for what he has read."	"You are not what you write, but what you have read."

Google is tackling the entire hardware/software ecosystem and "stack:" Its latest implementation, the one that won AlphaGo, runs on custom-designed ASICS Google calls its "Tensor Processing Unit:"[122]

> We also have a close working relationship with Google's datacenter and hardware platforms teams, which has allowed us to have significant input on the design and deployment of machine configurations that work well for machine learning (e.g., clusters of machines that have many GPUs and significant cross-machine bandwidth), as well as the requirements for Google's Tensor Processing Unit (TPU), a custom ASIC designed explicitly with neural network computations in mind and offering an order of magnitude performance and performance-per-watt improvement over other solutions.

> The Tensor Processing Unit is used in production for many kinds of models, including those used in ranking documents for every search query, and the use of many TPUs was also a key aspect of the recent AlphaGo victory over Lee Sedol in Seoul, Korea, in March 2016.

Now, I'm not a triumphalist about the potential of technology to change our profession and world of work. (To begin with, I'm a 6'1", 150 pound, blond-haired human being, not silicon and software.)

But I do believe that flat-footed assertions that machines could never do X or could never do Y are on the wrong side of history. The ultimate limits of human ingenuity and its ability to create tools---motivated by problems crying out for a better solution—remain unexplored and undefined.

Give the machines time. Maybe less time than you think.

---

22   Id.

"In capitalist reality as distinguished from its textbook picture, it is not [classical] . . . competition which counts but the competition from the new commodity, the new technology the new type of organization–competition which commands a decisive cost or quality advantage and which strikes not at the margins of the profits and the outputs of the existing firms but at their foundations and their very lives."

—Joseph Schumpeter, Capitalism, Socialism and Democracy (Harper & Rowe: New York, 1942 3d edition 1950) at 82

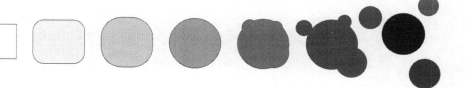

The Dynamics of Market Evolution

A widespread fallacy supposes that markets shift to new models primarily for rational reasons, when a clearly superior alternative arises, and similarl that firms participating in those markets change of their own volition, pursuing their own freely chosen purpose, and alter how they operate and what goods and services they provide because they have developed and are pursuing the intention to move resolutely in a specific new direction.

Were it so simple.

Markets, or macro systems, don't glide seamlessly from one equilibrium to another; they lurch. Some participants evince dissatisfaction with the prior model the very first moment it begins to creak, while many more apply temporary and provisional fixes in hopes the patient will recover and return to normal if only one can buy some time. At some point— assuming the market does indeed move to a new equilibrium and doesn't simply erode into irrelevance and oblivion—the patches and defects in the old model become so overwhelming that the weight of practice and actual choice, if not entirely opinion and personal preference, swings over to the new approach.

The theme of this closing chapter will be to describe the actual path—the dynamics, if you will—that markets and the firms within those markets typically follow when transformative change is afoot. I take as our texts, and will rely heavily upon, Thomas Kuhn's *Structure of Scientific Revolutions,*[123] and Albert Hirschman's *Exit, Voice, and Loyalty:*[124] Kuhn to provide the framework for macro, market wide changes, and Hirschman to lend insight into how organizations that fall into suboptimal behavior patterns (for example, because they're reluctant to adapt to marketplace changes) recover and return to high performance—or don't.

If any or all of the scenarios I've laid out is to materialize and change Law Land at a fundamental level, we have to get there from here. So it seems fitting to conclude with a discussion of how that actually tends to come about, both from the market wide perspective and within individual firms

---

123   Henceforth "Structure:" Chicago: University of Chicago Press, 1962, 4th edition, 2012

124   The full title is *Exit, Voice, and Loyalty: Responses to Decline in Firms, Organizations, and States,* henceforth "Exit, Voice & Loyalty:" Cambridge: Harvard University Press: 1970

or purposes of what follows, it doesn't matter whether you're putting your
₁oney on nothing changes, or on psychology and partnership, talent and
ee agency, differentiation, networks, new entrants, brands, machines—or
combination and mixture of your own devising. I believe it's valuable
₁ end *Tomorrowland* with a discussion and analysis of how we might
₁avigate across the divide to there from today. If we can't do that, all the
:enarios will remain trapped in hypothetical amber.

• • •

uhn published Structure more than half a century ago and Hirschman's
xit, Voice & Loyalty is coming up on that same mark, so you might fear
₁at they're dusty or have been superseded by more recent events and more
₁rrent learning. Don't be. I chose them because they have endured, and
₁deed their reputations have grown with the passage of time.

{ence a bit of background on each work and its author before we apply
₁eir frameworks to potential futures for Law Land.

₁n the occasion of the 50th anniversary of the publication of *Structure* a
:w years ago, the *Guardian* published a retrospective on the book's impact
₁d found, among other things, that despite a slow start, selling fewer
₁an 1,000 copies in the first year after its publication, it has grown into a
erennial must-read, with over 1.4 million copies printed; that a Google
:arch for it "returns more than 10 million hits;" that it's cited in well over
8,000 books available on Amazon; and that it's also one of the "most cited
ooks of all time" in academe.[125]

xit, *Voice & Loyalty* has also grown in stature (along with Hirschman's
wn reputation—it's commonly observed that the only reason he never
'on a Nobel is that he was so perplexingly difficult to categorize as a
₁inker) and is used to elucidate everything from how inner city gangs
₁aintain loyalty to the manipulative brilliance of frequent flier programs

---

25   "Thomas Kuhn: The man who changed the way the world looked at science,"
^e *Guardian,* August 19, 2012: at: https://www.theguardian.com/science/2012/aug/19/
₁omas-kuhn-structure-scientific-revolutions

and the predilection towards ever-more-radical polarization between America's two major political parties.[126]

If you're not familiar with *Structure*, in a nutshell it changed the way we think about progress in science. Before Kuhn, the assumption was that the sciences were working smoothly and essentially without interruption towards greater and greater understanding of the ways and the laws of the natural world, yielding ever greater descriptive accuracy and forecasting precision. While there were certainly marked and conspicuous advances—Kuhn spends time on the shift from Ptolemy to Copernicus and from Newton to quantum mechanics, for example—the fundamental trajectory of the sciences was continuous.

Kuhn led us to think otherwise.

Perhaps Kuhn was suited to upend what we assumed we knew about how science progresses since he was himself a physicist—and reflecting on how science progresses was not supposed to be a job for scientists themselves, it was meant to be reserved to those toiling in the history of ideas.

Kuhn's seminal insight came when the reform-oriented Harvard President James Conant assigned him to teach about the sciences for humanities students. For the first time, he dove into Aristotle at a deep level, asking himself essentially "how much of mechanics had Aristotle left unspecified or unknown, for Galileo and Newton and others to discover." Kuhn was shocked to learn that

---

126   I won't bore you with extended reviews, but here are a few to give you a flavor:

- Changes how you see the world. It illuminates yesterday, today, and tomorrow...His most important [book]. (Cass Sunstein *New York Review o Books* 2013-05-23)
- A 126-page burst of lucidity...[His] masterwork. (Roger Lowenstein *Wall Street Journal* 2013-03-22)
- One of the masterpieces of contemporary political thought. (Malcolm Gladwell *New Yorker* 2012-07-30)
- A marvelously perceptive essay which illuminates some of the most interesting economic and social questions of our time. I have read it with enormous interest and admiration, and the further pleasure that one has in being with an author who can think things through. (John Kenneth Galbraith)

as I was reading him, Aristotle appeared not only ignorant of mechanics, but a dreadfully bad physical scientist as well. About motion, in particular, his writings seemed to me full of egregious errors, both of logic and of observation.[127]

esistant to the notion that Aristotle might have been something of n idiot about mechanics—the Aristotelian view had been gospel for enturies, after all—Kuhn sought a different explanation and found by realizing that one can't truly understand Aristotle's science ʳithout understanding the intellectual tradition he worked within and ʳhich he and all his colleagues and followers took for granted as the ir they breathed.

ᴺewton and Galileo differed from Aristotle not just in their view of what motion," for example, means (change in position of a physical body ᵒ Newton and Galileo, pretty much any sort of change whatsoever to ᵣistotle), but in their bedrock intellectual framework.

ᵪccording to Kuhn, the structure of scientific revolutions has the following ᵣajectory (the italicized words are Kuhn's terms of art): A more or ᵉss lengthy period of *normal science* premised upon a widely accepted *ᵤaradigm* and devoted to *puzzle-solving* begins to encounter a series of *ⁿomalies* which cannot be explained within the standard framework ᵗen in place. As the anomalies proliferate and practitioners struggle ⁿsuccessfully to tweak the existing paradigm to accommodate them, a *ᵣisis* stage is eventually reached which is resolved by a *revolution* adopting new paradigm.

ᵒ stated, Kuhn's 200+-page volume may seem simplistic or too pat, ᵘut that may be mostly a reflection on how thoroughly his views have ᵉrmeated our world.

ᵒ that point, when Kuhn, writing in 1962, invoked the word "paradigm" ᵗ turned out he was single-handedly changing the currency of the word, ᵒ that a reader today attaches very different connotations to it than Kuhn ᵥas calling forth over 50 years ago. (And you are forbidden to use the ᵥithered phrase, "paradigm shift.") Later Kuhn himself wrote that the ᵒncept behind "paradigm" was "what I now take to be the most novel and

---

least understood aspect of this book," and suggested the word "exemplar" in its place. He ultimately admitted he has "lost control of the word," and abandoned it entirely.

This is how Kuhn described crossing from the old paradigm to the new:

> The transition from a paradigm in crisis to a new one from which a new tradition of normal science can emerge is far from a cumulative process, one achieved by an articulation or extension of the old paradigm. Rather it is a reconstruction of the field from new fundamentals, a reconstruction that changes some of the field's most elementary theoretical generalizations as well as many of its paradigm methods and applications. During the transition period there will be a large but never complete overlap between th problems that can be solved by the old and by the new paradigm. But there will also be a decisive difference in the modes of solution When the transition is complete, the profession will have changed its view of the field, its methods, and its goals.[128]

With humility, I submit Kuhn is describing something very similar to what Law Land may be on the threshold of entering. A business model—call it the Cravath System for simple ease of reference—that has served us amazingly well for a solid century and more, is beginning to creak. Of course, whether it's merely "creaking" or whether it's at risk of spontaneously disintegrating is a judgment that can only be reached by each of you for yourselves.

By "Cravath System," I refer not only to the recruitment/training/retention promotion system Paul Cravath designed and systematized, but to the entire business model of Big Law, which includes the following elements:

- The associate/partner dichotomy,

- The billable hour revenue model, grounded in cost of production rather than value to client,

- The utter asymmetry of risk between law firm (paid no matter the outcome) and client (bearing the outcome),

- The premise of every partner an owner with a legitimate voice, and

---

128   *Structure*, pp. 84–85.

- The subordination, dismissal, and demeaning of business professionals as "non-lawyers."

Where are the clients?

You could be forgiven for wondering where clients enter into all of this, as so far I've discussed them only tangentially and in passing. Fair enough. And it would be quite beside the point to note that this book declares itself all about "*law firms* beyond the horizon" and leave it simplistically and unhelpfully at that.

My firm belief, my life's learning, and hence my approach as reflected in this book stem from the reality that clients are embedded in everything that happens. Markets have two sides, and neither side unilaterally determines anything. If forced to condense how I view the balance between buyers and sellers to a phrase, I would nominate "Firms propose, clients dispose."

Less aphoristically, firms (suppliers) are free to offer whatever they wish into the market, but clients vote with their wallets, following their preferences, and with distressing finality for firms behind the curve, will defect to superior offerings.[129]

That clients will move to what they believe is superior is, you will recognize and I admit, a tautology. Markets can fail in many well-recognized ways:

- Failures of and shortcomings in disclosure are a classic—securities disclosure laws were built around trying to fix this—meaning that clients could be misinformed and misled. In Law Land, with sophisticated clients, this isn't systemic.

- Externalities are another classic mode of market failure, where market participants can single-handedly impose costs (or less controversially benefits) on parties outside the market. A factory wantonly dumping waste into the air and water is the classic

---

129   Silicon Valley startups have introduced notions such as "fail fast," "pivot," "iterate," and "minimum viable product" into the vocabulary of the larger business world, and even if you think these terms have something of an offensive self-congratulatory tone about them, I suggest they all are sincere attempts to grapple with the marketplace reality that clients—and not primarily firms—cast the ultimate votes on what succeeds and what fails.

example, but also points the way to solving the problem of social costs becoming disconnected from market costs—tax or regulate the externality-generating behavior. In Law Land, hard to imagine how *economic* externalities would arise.

- Most interestingly for our purposes, failures of collective action. Thi somewhat oblique phrase refers to markets trapped in a dynamic where everyone would be better off in the long run if everyone behaved differently, but also where it remains in each individual actor's rational self-interest to keep acting in the same way unless and until everyone else changes.[130] This might have some real teeth in Law Land, as implied in Chapter VII, Brands Win. But if demonstrably superior offerings enter the market, it will only be a matter of time.

But barring a form of market failure, clients are the dominant arbiters of what offerings win.

Let me be more explicit: When Apple introduced the iPhone, how much weight in the marketplace did BlackBerry's preference for the status quo ante carry? Customers had other ideas.

Lore has it that Peter Drucker would occasionally stump his business students with the question, "What is *the one thing* that every firm has to have?" Students would volunteer "Cash?," "Workers?," "A product or service?," "A market?," none of which Drucker was looking for. He was looking for this one thing: Clients.

So in closing this brief interlude on clients, let me admit what may be an intellectual shortcoming: I have sometimes found the recent discovery of the power of clients, a subject of widespread and popular debate in Law Land, odd. To my mind, clients have always had tremendous power. Wha may indeed be new is that now they know it, and aren't retiring about exercising it.

It's actually deeper than that.

---

130   Those of you interested in learning more about this could do no better than to look up Stanford Economic Professor and 2012 winner of the Nobel Prize in Economics Alvin Roth's *Who Gets What—and Why: The new economics of matchmaking and marke design* (Houghton Mifflin: New York): 2015. Disclosure: Al is a friend of Adam Smith, Esq

sking "where are the clients?" and framing the answer in terms of a yin/
ang or push/pull between clients as one set of players on one side and
rms as another set of players on the other side misapprehends markets at
profound level. Clients and firms alike are suffused into and permeate
ie entirety of the market dynamic; they cannot be separated in any way
iat has meaning or aids understanding of who is supposedly acting
n whom.

challenge you to describe any major market shift resulting from the
nilateral actions and preferences of clients or of firms. Starbucks must
ave believed that it could offer better coffee than Howard Johnson's or
ie local corner diner, but customers had to take them up on it. We know
Vestern Union believed telegrams were the last word in long-distance
ommunication and that this new-fangled telephone was too complicated
nd chancy; customers decided otherwise. (We know this because
lexander Graham Bell offered his nationwide US patents on the telephone
Western Union; they declined.)

[ot just products or services that succeed but those that fail and those
iat come into existence from nothingness exhibit the same symbiotic
rm→client→firm→client endless loop. According to all accounts,
Aotorola really *did* introduce the most sophisticated and capable calling
etwork in the world with Iridium, but it filed spectacularly for bankruptcy
1 1999 a year after launching its globe-spanning satellite network.
Customers were happier with what they had.

o with all the scenarios here. Whichever come to pass and to what
xtent will not be determined by firms' offering whatever they believe
the market" needs most, nor by clients' instructing firms exactly what to
roduce, or else. The evolution will be interactive, dynamic, uncertain, and
ontingent. But it doesn't help to mentally juxtapose clients and firms as
wo separate and marginally hostile camps.

Back to Kuhn, with a segue.

Scientific disciplines advance from one paradigm to another with no outsiders participating or looking over their shoulders. The scientists within the discipline make the call and collectively form the only opinion that matters.

Not so in economically vibrant disciplines like Law Land. What firms offer, and what clients flock to, is the result of a dialog and interaction, no a cloistered decision over what provides a superior description of nature. Any sane observer would have to assume that equilibria in commercial markets were very far afield indeed from Kuhn's thinking when he was composing *Structure*.

Yet his conceptual dynamic has endured, and remains the most potent description *and explanation* of how enormous belief systems comprising a multitude of independent players somehow manage to shift to an entirely new equilibrium position against—at least initially—the weight of all established authority, practice, and custom.

Structure's force and durability owe to its moving beyond description to (as I implied) explanation. The distinction is not abstruse. Ancients could describe, with tremendous accuracy, the timing of the rising and setting of the sun and the progression of the seasons, but they couldn't explain it beyond the charming but quaint and tautological story that the gods made it so, riding their chariots of fire across the sky and calling forth the budding spring and the fall harvest. ("Tautological" because "the gods did it" is scarcely removed from "the gods made the world that way" which is scarcely a step removed from "the world is that way.") It took a combination of Copernicus, Galileo, and Kepler to get us to an actual *explanation* of sunset and sunrise and the march of the seasons.

So too with Kuhn's *Structure*. Before, historians of science could describe and annotate to a fare-thee-well, say, the emerging constituency and consensus in favor of quantum mechanics over Newtonian supremacy, but they never quite accounted for exactly how the mass mindset shift occurred. And don't be tempted to assume that it's because the shiny new theory elucidates anything and everything observable while the tarnished

ld theory can only shed light on pieces of reality. No theory is complete;
1ey are all works in progress.

uhn himself warned us to be on guard against this facile assumption:

> No theory ever solves all the puzzles with which it is confronted at
> a given time. If any and every failure to fit were ground for theory
> rejection, all theories ought to be rejected at all times.[131]

till, he explained how we can and do get there from here.

o with all that said, permit me to borrow again from Kuhn as he describes
1e array of reactions by professionals actually laboring in the very field
1 question as signs of the old model's senescence begin to appear. I
1spect you'll find it apt. Kuhn's model is subtle and multi-faceted, and
ot susceptible to condensed or summary treatment if one wants fairly
1troduce his thinking to the novitiate or take those who've read Kuhn
1rough my application of *Structure* to Law Land.

irst, Kuhn's description of how (say) the Cravath System
ecomes dominant:[132]

> When, in the development of a natural science, an individual or
> group first produces a synthesis able to attract most of the next
> generation's practitioners, the older schools gradually disappear. In
> part their disappearance is caused by their members' conversion to
> the new paradigm. But there are always some men who cling to one
> or another of the older views and they are simply read out of the
> profession, which thereafter ignores their work. The new paradigm
> implies a new and more rigid definition of the field. Those
> unwilling or unable to accommodate their work to it must proceed
> in isolation or attach themselves to some other group.[133]

'he next stage is when practitioners with the most acute horizon-scanning
adar, or the most instinctively curious, begin to wonder why the dominant

---

31   *Structure* at 146.

32   All quotes from *Structure*, emphasis supplied.

33   *Structure* at p. 19, "The Route to Normal Science"

worldview seems less effective at producing results in a few (perhaps backwater or arcane) areas than it used to be. Note that no one is yet questioning the dominant paradigm: It's just become noticeable that it's failing on a few peripheral counts where it used to succeed.

> Novelty ordinarily emerges only for the man who, knowing *with precision* what he should expect, is able to recognize that something has gone wrong. **Anomaly appears only against the background provided by the paradigm.** The more precise and far-reaching the paradigm is, the mores sensitive an indicator it provides of anomal and hence of an occasion for paradigm change.

> In the normal mode of discovery even resistance to change has a use. By ensuring that the paradigm will not be too easily surrendered, resistance guarantees that scientists will not be lightly distracted and that the anomalies that lead to paradigm change will penetrate existing knowledge to the core. The very fact that a significant scientific novelty so often emerges simultaneously from several laboratories is an index both to the strongly traditional nature of normal science and to the completeness with which that traditional pursuit prepares the way for its own change.[134]

Here Kuhn has described and specified that it's not that the dominant model encounters obstacles in the case of this or that specific firm or within subsets of the market, which could always be attributed to those firms' failures to implement it faithfully or the peculiar quirks of that subset of the market. Kuhn's point is that the model begins to break down system-wide and "often emerges simultaneously [in a wide number of firms]."

The next step deals with how people subscribing to the incumbent model begin to react to the appearance of chinks in the armor of the conventional business (or "normal science") model.

> The awareness of anomaly [has by now] lasted so long and penetrated so deep that one can appropriately describe the fields affected by it as in a state of growing crisis. Because it demands

---

134   *Structure* at p. 65, "Anomaly and the Emergence of Scientific Discoveries" (italics original, bold supplied)

large-scale paradigm destruction and major shifts in the problems and techniques of [the business model], the emergence of new theories is generally preceded by a period of pronounced professional insecurity. As one might expect, that insecurity is generated by the persistent failure of the puzzles of normal science to come out as they should. Failure of existing rules is the prelude to a search for new ones.[135]

Principles always become a matter of vehement discussion when practice is at an ebb."

—George Gissing (English novelist, 1857—1903)

he resident or incumbent business model doesn't go down without a ght, nor do its adherents. Indeed, they stick to their belief in the "Cravath ystem" (or Ptolemaic astronomy or Newtonian mechanics) they've ubscribed to all their professional lives with redoubled vehemence. Yes, ley may experiment with changes at the margin, but existential doubts out the validity of the fundaments are impermissible:

> Insofar as he is engaged in normal science, the research worker [lawyer] is a solver of puzzles, not a tester of paradigms. Though he may, during the search for a particular puzzle's solution, try out a number of alternative approaches, rejecting those that fail to yield the desired result, **he is not testing the *paradigm* when he does so.**
>
> Instead he is like the chess player who, with a problem stated and the board physically or mentally before him, tries out various alternative moves in the search for a solution. These trial attempts, whether by the chess player or by the scientist, are trials only of themselves, not of the rules of the game. They are possible only so long as the paradigm itself is taken for granted.
>
> Therefore, paradigm-testing occurs only after persistent failure to solve a noteworthy puzzle has given rise to crisis. And even then it occurs only after the sense of crisis has evoked an alternate candidate for paradigm. In [business and in] the sciences the testing situation never consists, as puzzle-solving does, simply in

35   *Structure* at 68, "Crisis and the Emergence of Scientific Theories"

the comparison of a single paradigm with nature. Instead **testing occurs as part of the competition between two rival paradigms for the allegiance of the scientific community.**[136]

Or in the famous and pithy expression of political wisdom, "you can't beat somebody with nobody."

This much makes ready sense to all of us; *of course* you don't jettison your existing business model unless and until you have a promising replacement.

Now we transition into Kuhn's most profound and also slippery concept: When one paradigm, or one business model, supplants another, the enormous difference between their two views of how the world works— which each brings with it of necessity—can mean that believers in one may not be able to understand what the other camp is saying. The meaning of language literally changes:

> Within the new paradigm, **old terms, concepts and experiments fall into new relationships one with the other.** The inevitable result is what we must call, though the term is not quite right, a misunderstanding between the two competing schools.[137]

Kuhn give us the examples of Einstein's model of space/time supplanting Euclid's, and of the Copernicus/Ptolemy transition.

> The laymen who scoffed at Einstein's general theory of relativity because space could not be "curved"—it was not that sort of thing—were not simply wrong or mistaken.

> Nor were the mathematicians, physicists, and philosophers who tried to develop a Euclidean version of Einstein's theory. What had previously been meant by space was necessarily flat, homogeneous, isotropic, and unaffected by the presence of matter. If it had not been, Newtonian physics would not have worked.

---

136   *Structure* at 144, "The Resolution of Revolutions" (italics original, bold supplied)

137   Id.

To make the transition to Einstein's universe, the whole conceptual web whose strands are space, time, matter, force, and so on, had to be shifted and laid down again on nature whole.

Only men who had together undergone or failed to undergo that transformation would be able to discover precisely what they agreed or disagreed about. Communication across the revolutionary divide is inevitably partial.

[Or] consider those who called Copernicus mad because he proclaimed that the earth moved. They were not just wrong or quite wrong. Part of what they meant by "earth" was fixed position. Their earth, at least, could not be moved.

Correspondingly, Copernicus' innovation was not simply to move the earth. Rather, it was a whole new way of regarding the problems of physics and astronomy, one that necessarily changed the meaning of both "earth" and "motion." Without those changes the concept of a moving earth was mad.[138]

1 other words, it's no exaggeration to say that people subscribing to one aradigm, or Law Land business model, and those subscribing to an tterly different business model, *do not understand what the other camp is ilking about.*

These examples point to the most fundamental aspect of the incommensurability of competing paradigms. In a sense that I am unable to explicate further, **the proponents of competing paradigms practice their trades in different worlds.**[139]

or my money, this is Kuhn's subtlest, and most profound and powerful, isight. It helps us understand why Law Land leaders, partners and aily foot soldiers, and those in the various other camps of belief and ractice—talent, differentiation, new entrants, networks, brands, machines, nd more—seem to be talking across a conceptual divide. They are. No onder communication sometimes fails.

---

38   Id.

39   *Structure* at pp. 148—151 (bold emphasis supplied, italics original)

And by no means does everyone make the transition:

> **How, then, are [people] brought to make this transposition? Par†**
> **of the answer is that they are very often not.**

> Copernicanism made few converts for almost a century after
> Copernicus' death. Newton's work was not generally accepted for
> more than half a century after the *Principia* appeared.

"Science proceeds one funeral at a time."

–Max Planc

Proponents of the new paradigm aren't blind to the magnitude of the
"incommensurable" divide they have staked out and defined.

> Darwin, in a particularly perceptive passage at the end of his *Origi*
> *of Species*, wrote: "**Although I am fully convinced of the truth**
> **of the views given in this volume…, I by no means expect to**
> **convince experienced naturalists whose minds are stocked with** **i**
> **multitude of facts all viewed, during a long course of years, from**
> **a point of view directly opposite to mine…**

> "But I look with confidence to the future,--to young and rising
> naturalists, who will be able to view both sides of the question
> with impartiality."

Kuhn's thinking is nuanced enough and his temperament sympathetic
enough that he not only forgives those who cannot vault the chasm but he
relocates the dialogue into another plane entirely. It's not something, he
says, that can be distilled in reductionist form to true and false, ancient an
modern, dwelling in the past vs. dwelling in the future.

> In the past [the difference of opinion] has most often been taken
> to indicate that scientists, being only human, cannot always admit
> their errors, even when confronted with strict proof.

I would argue, rather, that in these matters **neither proof nor error is at issue. The transfer of allegiance from paradigm to paradigm is a conversion experience that cannot be forced.**
Lifelong resistance, particularly from those whose productive careers have committed them to an older tradition of normal science, is not a violation of scientific standards. [...]

Inevitably, at times of revolution, that assurance seems stubborn and pigheaded as indeed it sometimes becomes.
But it is also something more.[140]

uhn cuts to the heart of how a science, or an industry, shifts from one ominant incumbent paradigm to another upstart contender when he quarely locates it in the dimension of faith and not the dimension of near reason.

But paradigm debates are not really about relative problem-solving ability, though for good reasons they are usually couched in those terms. Instead, the issue is which paradigm should in the future guide [the profession].

Those who embrace a new paradigm at an early stage must often do so in defiance of the evidence provided by problem-solving. He must, that is, have faith that the new paradigm will succeed with the many large problems that confront it, knowing only that the older paradigm has failed with a few. A decision of that kind can only be made on faith.

... Crisis alone is not enough. There must also be a basis, though it need be neither rational nor ultimately correct, for faith in the particular candidate chosen. Something must make at least a few scientists feel that the new proposal is on the right track, and **sometimes it is only personal and inarticulate aesthetic considerations that can do that.** ...

This is not to suggest that new paradigms triumph ultimately through some mystical aesthetic. On the contrary, very few men desert a tradition for these reasons alone... But there is no single

---

40   *Structure* at 157.

argument that can or should persuade them all. Rather than a single group conversion, what occurs is an increasing shift in the distribution of professional allegiances.[141]

Likewise within firms and organizations themselves: Transformations are never self-executing, frictionless, and driven purely by what logic in the light of circumstances would dictate.

• • •

Enter Albert Hirschman.

Born in Berlin in 1915; fled the Nazis in 1933; studied in Paris, London, and Trieste; joined the anti-Mussolini resistance; fought with the Republicans in the Spanish Civil War; served in the French Army until the country's collapse in 1940; helped to organize an underground railway for Jewish and other refugees out of France into Spain over the Pyrenees; emigrated to America; joined the US Army; was a translator at Nuremberg; worked at the Fed; followed that with a succession of academic appointments in economics departments at Yale (1956–1958), Columbia (1958–1964), Harvard (1964–1974) and the Institute for Advanced Study (1974–until his death in 2012 at age 97).

Exit, Voice & Loyalty, published in 1970, is all of 126 pages long, and hinges around Hirschman's analysis of what options people have when an organization they're loyal to suffers a perceived decline in quality or pursues a route the individual disagrees with. The primary options an individual can exercise are "exit" (withdraw, as an employee resigning or a customer taking their business elsewhere) or "voice" (expressing one's views and opinions and hoping to influence the organization's behavior). The two aren't mutually exclusive, although obviously turning the threat of exit into reality usually truncates the voice conversation.

---

141   *Structure* at 157.

he book was immediately received as a "burst of lucidity, whose [insights]
ere readily apparent,"[142] and it has remained in print, selling steadily, for
early 50 years.

irschman set himself the task of describing the details of how
rganizations change by postulating a firm or a system that had lapsed
to suboptimal patterns of behavior and asking the simple question,
What might happen next? Who might exert influence and how would
ey do that?"

ere's his premise:

> Under any economic, social, or political system, individuals,
> business firms, and organizations in general are subject to lapses
> from efficient, rational, law-abiding, virtuous, or otherwise
> functional behavior. [Such] failures are bound to occur, if only for
> all kinds of accidental reasons.[143]

irschman is sympathetic and ready to recognize that "fault" often has
othing to do with why firms begin lagging their peers. He could have
ritten this, although he most assuredly did not, with Law Land in mind:

> Precisely in sectors where there are large numbers of firms
> competing with one another in similar conditions, declines in
> the fortunes of individual firms are just as likely to be due to
> random, subjective factors that are reversible or remediable as to
> permanent adverse shifts in cost and demand conditions. In these
> circumstances, mechanisms of recuperation would play a most
> useful role in avoiding social losses as well as human hardship.[144]

ut these "mechanisms of recuperation" don't operate equally across the
embers of an industry. Firms farther down the food chain respond
ifferently and have a distinct set of options compared to firms at the top
f the ladder. Note how Hirschman differentiates between how clients

---

2   Roger Lowenstein, *The Choice: To Squawk or to Go:*, The Wall Street Journal
arch 22, 2013, at: http://www.wsj.com/articles/SB10001424127887323869604578370?
034963414

3   Exit, Voice & Loyalty, *Introduction and Doctrinal Background,* at 1.

4   Id. at 3.

respond to deterioration in the services of high-, medium-, and low-quality firms:

> If one assumes a complete and continuous array of varieties, from cheap and poor quality to expensive and high quality [a fair approximation of Law Land], then deterioration of any but the top and bottom variety will rapidly lead to a combination of exits: **the quality-consumers move to the higher-price, higher-quality products and the price-conscious ones go over to the lower-price lower-quality varieties;** the former will still tend to get out first when it is quality that declines rather than price that rises but the latter will not be far behind.[145]

Here Hirschman has articulated the dynamics of why the Hollow Middle is a place no firm wants to be. What does it take for "exit" to kick in at the high end?

> If only because of economies of scale, it is plausible that density is lower in the upper ranges of quality than in the lower and middle ranges. If this is so, then **deterioration of a product in the upper quality ranges has to be fairly substantial before the quality-conscious will exit** and switch to the next better variety. Hence the scope for, and resort, to voice option will be greatest in these ranges; it will be comparatively slight in the medium- and low-quality ranges.[146]

That describes how clients react to changes in quality and/or price. What about the lawyers at the firm themselves? Hirschman says, in accordance with our intuition, that it depends on how easy it is for a lawyer to "exit:"

> What happens to voice in organizations where the price of exit is high? Some tentative suggestions can be advanced by distinguishing between those high-exit-price organizations where the price of entry is zero (because, as in the case of the family or nation one enters them as a result of one's birth) and those where this price is high as well.

---

145   Exit, Voice & Loyalty at 52, bold emphasis supplied

146   Id. at 53, bold emphasis supplied.

For the latter organizations it has just been shown that the onset of felt discontent and therefore of voice will be delayed. Since the high price of exit does away, on the other hand, with the threat of exit as an effective instrument of voice, these organizations (...) **will often be able to repress both voice and exit. In the process, they will largely deprive themselves of both recuperation mechanisms.**[147]

rom the ninth and final chapter, *The Elusive Optimal Mix of Exit and ɔice* (pp. 120 et seq.), I have reproduced and adapted Hirschman's ble (below), which he describes as "by way of a very rough summary," ɪd "a somewhat schematic finale" "in view of the numerous baroque ɪnamentations which have been added."

ere's my mild reformulation of Hirschman's typology:

- **Top left**: Organizations where **both exit and voice** play important roles; these are relatively few, and Hirschman specifically notes that "there is no implication that the organizations which are equipped with both feedback mechanisms are necessarily more advanced or viable than those which rely primarily on one alone. All depends on the responsiveness of the organization."

- **Bottom left:** Traditional human groups from which **exit** is virtually unheard of (for example, your family or your birth religion) while **voice** is to some degree available.

- **Top right:** Here Hirschman places most "competitive business enterprises [that is to say, most businesses in approximations of perfectly competitive markets]" and I echo by pinning most law firms in the same quadrant, vis-à-vis both their clients and their own lawyers. It's not news that the first choice of clients and lawyers alike who are critical of a firm's behavior and performance is simply to leave. Life is short and we all have a surfeit of options.

The interesting question from the firm's perspective is whether it is sensitive to these exits: Does it heed their implicit warning and respond with reforms or does it overlook them or plow straight

---

47   Id. at 97, bold emphasis supplied.

ahead regardless, reassuring itself that the departures can all be laid at the door of (variously) malcontents, impossible perfectionists, or the obtuse and uncomprehending?

In a separate table, which I will spare you my reproducing here, Hirschman offers examples of types of organizations where decline primarily prompts exit but the signal is ignored, and it's unflattering company indeed:

- o "Public enterprise subject to competition from an alternative mode" (think public schools facing charters),
- o "Lazy oligopolists" (ouch),
- o "Corporation-shareholder relations," and
- o "Inner cities" (double ouch).

- Finally, we have the nastiest quadrant of all, firms at the **bottom right**, deaf to any and all messages, which Hirschman confirms is no place to be: "Exit is here considered as treason and voice as mutiny. Such organizations are likely to be less viable, in the long run, than the others [since] exit and voice will be engaged in only when deterioration has reached so advanced a stage that recovery is no longer either possible or desirable. Moreover, at this stage, voice and exit will be undertaken with such strength that their effect will be destructive rather than reformist."

My adaptation of Hirschman's table follows, to which I have added my own suggestions of what types of law firms might fall in each cell. If you're tempted to engage in the exercise of mapping your own firm onto one of the quadrants, please be my guest. The only rule is that you must perform that exercise with undiluted self-awareness and candor.

Exit and Voice: Voluntary associations, political parties, and some businesses such as those selling to a few buyers—*only the most highly attuned and responsive law firms*	Exit, not Voice: Competitive businesses with many customers—*most law firms vis-à-vis clients and their own lawyers*
Voice, not Exit: Family, tribe, nation, church—*the idealized partnership of our dreams?*	Neither Exit nor Voice: Parties in totalitarian one-party systems, terror groups, gangs—*law firms impervious to dissent*

o recapitulate: Our Platonic ideal partnership would be highly responsive
o "voice"—expressed dissatisfaction of clients and/or lawyers, but
elatively immune to exit. Partners view themselves as there for life,
nd clients' institutional loyalty is strong enough to endure temporary
isappointment. But the firm really listens.

t the opposite extreme we have firms magisterially indifferent to client
omplaints and departures, as well as to complaints from and resignations
f their own partners. These promise to be, as Hirschman delicately puts
, "less viable in the long run."

he majority of law firms, however, probably congregate in the top right,
where they don't really listen to their clients or even their own lawyers
ery much—not, certainly, if "listening" implies acting upon what you
ave heard and not simply receiving it passively (and impassively). Rather
hockingly—and in a pattern of behavior that would be inconceivable
n other sophisticated professional service arenas such as management
onsulting or investment banking—the vast majority of law firms don't
ven ask clients who've departed what went wrong or what the firm could
ave done differently. (This assumes the law firm is even aware the client is
one in the first place.[148])

'Nothing has an uglier look than reason, when it is not on our side."

–Lord Halifax (George Savile, 1st Marquis of Halifax (1633 – 1695))

t remains to inquire how law firms, facing some or all of the scenarios I've
aid out, will adapt. My greatest fear, as a lifelong participant in and analyst
f Law Land, is that they will fail to cope.

Iow could that be possible?, you may fairly ask. Separately or
umulatively, many of these conceivable tomorrow's have less space for

---

48   At an executive education forum held at Harvard Law's *Center on the Legal
rofession* a couple of years ago, which I was attending as a guest lecturer, the then GC
f Viacom, who had been a partner at Milbank, let loose a tirade about law firms who
latantly overbilled. An audience member asked what he did about an offending firm. "I
ay the bill, and I never use them again." "Do the firms call to find out what happened?"
Never; not once, not ever."

Law Land, or entail a Law Land operating with drastically constricted financial freedom, success, and power. How could law firms *not* respond?

We conclude, fittingly, with Hirschman again. In his 1991 *Rhetoric of Reaction: Perversity, futility, jeopardy*[149] he surveyed reactionary thought in response to the French Revolution and the Declaration of the Rights of Man, to the 19th Century's universal suffrage movements, and to the 20th Century's welfare state, and in each case identified and described three principal arguments invoked against change:

- Perversity: change will harm the very people it's intended to benefit In other words, no substitute for Big Law will be viable, reliable, or effective; clients who flee to alternatives will be sorely disappointed. The Law of Unintended Consequences strikes with a vengeance.

- Futility: the problems the new models may be trying to address are s deep-rooted and fundamental that nothing can be changed. In othe words, Big Law may not be perfect, but its track record of more than a century of success proves it has arrived at the optimum model that can realistically be achieved. The status quo will prove impregnable.

- Jeopardy: any change will endanger previous hard-won accomplishments and will come at unacceptable cost. In other words, attacking the foundations of Big Law could be tantamount to attacking the foundations of justice itself.

I would be the last to put it beyond the skills, or the will, of Law Land to invoke all these time-tested reactionary rhetorical devices and then some.

One can envision a further trajectory starting at dismissive and condescending, moving through anger and denial, crossing into desperate attempts to strike alliances, partnerships, and bargains with the forces of change, and ending no one can predict where.

Then again, history has delivered its verdict of vindication on the Rights of Man, universal suffrage, and the compassionate state, and that verdict is final.

May we hope history is kind to law firms.

---

149   Belknap Press/The President and Fellows of Harvard College: Cambridge, 199

But history doesn't hearken to hope; it hearkens to action.

Afterword

And it is fortunate for men to be in a situation in which, though their passions may prompt them to be wicked, they have nevertheless an interest in not being so."

—Montesquieu, De esprit de lois, XXI, 20 (The Spirit of the Laws)
1748.150

In the late 20th Century, the always unexpected Albert Hirschman, along with other scholars, revived the notion of *doux commerce,* first enunciated and elaborated in the 1700s by, among others, Adam Smith himself, Condorcet, Hume, Montesquieu, and others.[150] The doux commerce thesis comes close to positing that market economies would be worth having for their own sake—for the beneficent influence they have on human behavior—even if they were less than optimal at production and distribution.

Its emergence can be traced to French Enlightenment reaction against Bourbon autocracy, but the Dutch and the British enlightenment liberals soon adopted it and oversaw its maturation. A 1704 "technical text on commerce" says "Commerce attaches [men] to one another through mutual utility."[151] It follows somewhat logically from the presupposition that in a market economy, many if not all of your transactions are mutually beneficial exchanges voluntarily entered into—but they in turn presuppose a base level of trust, honor, and courtesy. Per Hirschman: Commerce is "a powerful moralizing agent which brings many nonmaterial improvements to society, even though a bit of hypocrisy may have to be accepted into the bargain."

150   For a friendly and approachable overview, I recommend Hirschman, *The Passions and the Interests: Political Arguments For Capitalism Before Its Triumph* (Princeton, NJ: Princeton University Press, 1977)

151   "Magic, Maths, and Money: the relationship between science and finance," *What doux-commerce means to me,* 2 August 2013: http://magic-maths-money.blogspot.com/2013/08/what-doux-commerce-means-to-me.html

And he quotes Samuel Ricard (translated from the French):

> Commerce attaches [men] one to another through mutual utility.
> Through commerce the moral and physical passions are supersede
> by interest...Commerce has a special character which distinguishes
> it from all other professions. It affects the feelings of men so
> strongly that it makes him who was proud and haughty suddenly
> turn supple, bending and serviceable. Through commerce, man
> learns to deliberate, to be honest, to acquire manners, to be pruder
> and reserved in both talk and action. Sensing the necessity to be
> wise and honest in order to succeed, he flees vice, or at least his
> demeanor exhibits decency and seriousness so as not to arouse
> any adverse judgement [sic] on the part of present and future
> acquaintances; he would not dare make a spectacle of himself for
> fear of damaging his credit standing and thus society may well
> avoid a scandal which it might otherwise have to deplore.

Thomas Paine, a more profound thinker than he's often given credit
for, wrote in his *Rights of Man* (1792), "[Commerce] is a pacific system,
operating to cordialise mankind."

Lest you think the thesis archaic or quaint, modern game theory has
validated it just in the past couple of decades.

> Tullock (1997) works out Smith's insight in light of modern game
> theory. In a five-sided, single-play game where players must choose
> between "cooperate" and "defect," all players chose the "defect"
> response, resulting in a prisoners' dilemma.

> However, when the game was played repeatedly and players
> were allowed to form groups and communicate freely, all players
> chose the "cooperate" response. Tullock argues that their change
> in response is due to the reputation effect. "Anyone who chose
> to defect in any given game would, in essence, put himself in a
> situation where it would be extremely difficult for him to get
> partners for any future game" (p. 23).

He adds that the reason that the prisoners' dilemma disappears under repeated plays is "simply that people voluntarily choose their own partners" (pp. 23-24). The ability to choose one's playing partner, says Tullock, adds a "don't play" option to the above two-strategy game. The "don't play" option raises the expected cost of cheating. Thus, he concludes, "a reputation for being 'sound' is a valuable asset, and we should expect people to make every effort to get it" (p. 25).[152]

Moving from the abstract plane of multi-player game theory to a real world study:

> A reputation for fair dealing is necessary for a roofer whose trade is limited to a town with a population of fifty thousand. One bad roof and he is finished in Iowa City, and so he practices virtue with care. By now he would not put on a bad roof even if he could get away with it.[153]

Completing our cook's tour of the pedigree of doux commerce, I can't resist citing Adam Smith's observation: He noted that the Dutch, then the most commercial nation in the world, "are also the most faithful to their word," and he hoped this honesty would build in the English and Scottish, not quite as commercially advanced at the time but in Smith's view and experience second to the Dutch in commercial probity and fair dealing.

Don't take this as an offense against political correctness: Not for a moment did Smith attribute "faithful[ness] to the word" to national character. He was convinced it was reducible, in the most complimentary way, to self-interest.

> "When a person makes perhaps 20 contracts in a day, he cannot gain so much by endeavouring to impose on his neighbours, as the very appearance of a cheat would make him lose."

---

152   *Planning & Markets,* III. Moral Choice in the Private Property Order (University of Southern California: Los Angeles, 1999) , at http://www-pam.usc.edu/volume6/6i1a2s3.html

153   Id.

The most self-defeating thing a merchant can do would be to jeopardize their reputation in the eyes of those with whom they wish to "truck, barter and exchange"—a propensity he believed inherent in human nature. Smith concludes that "whenever commerce is introduced into any country probity and punctuality always accompany it."[154]

You didn't know you had picked up a book about doux commerce, and you have not.

I close with it, however, because it symbolizes to me the highest value of capitalism, free markets, and modern liberal economies. It is not because they enrich us all, or can do if we get distribution right—it's because in no trivial sense they ennoble our everyday lives.

We have seen its potent and pervasive impact in every recent corner of human history since our emergence from feudalism, from the pre-War ghettoes of Eastern Europe to small town America today, and it continues to vindicate what is doubtless one of Adam Smith's most widely recognized lines, the sentence with which he opens *Theory of Moral Sentiments*:

> How selfish soever man may be supposed, there are evidently some principles in his nature, which interest him in the fortune of others and render their happiness necessary to him, though he derives nothing from it except the pleasure of seeing it.

I have tried to show some of the ways this plays out in the world to our endless amazement, delight, and enrichment. And it is to these intrinsic

---

154   The fuller quote in context is:

> This division of labour, from which so many advantages are derived, is not originally the effect of any human wisdom, which foresees and intends that general opulence to which it gives occasion. It is the necessary, though very slow and gradual consequence of a certain propensity in human nature which has in view no such extensive utility; the propensity to truck, barter, and exchange one thing for another.

> Whether this propensity be one of those original principles in human nature, of which no further account can be given; or whether, as seems more probable, it be the necessary consequence of the faculties of reason and speech it belongs not to our present subject to enquire. It is common to all men.

Wealth of Nations, Book I, Chapter II ("Of the Principle which Gives Occasion to the Division of Labor.")

uman values, which square *Moral Sentiments* with *Wealth of Nations* and hich echo the best traditions of some of the great religions, to which I ave devoted the recent arc of my career, and this book.

Author's Note & Acknowledgments

It's customary, and right and seemly so to do, for authors to devote a note to acknowledging their debts to their professional colleagues, wise friends, and the unexpectedly accosted, who have contributed time and thoughts and substance to the work you're reading.

My turn.

I'm often asked how much time I spent writing, be it composing a column or writing a book. The factual answer is, "I wouldn't dream of keeping track," but the truthful answer is, "Figuring out what you want to say is the tough and time-consuming part; writing it down from there is easy."

These are some of the people who've helped me figure out what I wanted to say:

- Wim Dejonghe, Senior Partner, and Richard Punt, Chief Executive Officer of Peerpoint, Allen & Overy;

- Matthew Layton, Managing Partner, and Bas Boris Visser, Global Head of Innovation and Business Change, Clifford Chance;

- Piet Meeter, Global Leader, Deloitte Legal Services;

- Peter Kalis, Chairman & Global Managing Partner, K&L Gates;

- Robert Couture, Executive Director, McGuire Woods;

- Ray Bayley and Lois Haubold, Co-Founders, NovusLaw;

- Brad Karp. Chair, Paul Weiss;

- Joe Lecesse, Managing Partner, Proskauer;

- Alex Hamilton, RadiantLaw;

- Karl Chapman, CEO, and Andy Daws, Vice President, North America Riverview Law;

- Ralph Baxter, Chairman of the Advisory Board, Thomson Reuters Legal Executive Institute.

Ve all live in a dense web of social, cultural, historical, intellectual, literary, nd—yes—economic, traditions and intersecting networks. As I began to ork through conceiving and then creating this book over the past year or ɔ I became newly aware of how embedded we all are in those networks nd how much of our curiosity, our proclivities, our capacities, and ltimately our reach, are defined and circumscribed by their gentle and enevolent grasp upon us.

o above all I must acknowledge that I am heir to a profound and enerous, richly provocative and still vibrant, intellectual tradition. May I e a small foot soldier in the endless human quest to enrich what we think ɔout our world.

Index

Bibliography

A framework for legal sourcing, Radiant Law, (June 23, 2016), http://www. radiantlaw.com/blog/a-framework-for-legal-sourcing/.

Adam Smith, An Inquiry into the Nature and Causes of the Wealth of Nations, Book 1, Chapter 1, (London, 1776; The Modern Library: New York 1994).

Adam Smith, The Theory of Moral Sentiments I:79 (London, 1759).

Adam Smith, Wealth of Nations, Book I, Chapter II (1904).

Albert Hirschman, Exit, Voice, Loyalty: Responses to Decline in Firms, (Cambridge: Harvard University Press: 1970).

Albert O. Hirschman, The Passions and the Interests: Political Arguments for Capitalism Before its Triumph, (Princeton, NJ: Princeton University Press, 1977).

Albert O. Hirschman, The Rhetoric of Reaction: Perversity, Futility, Jeopardy, (Belknap Press/The President and Fellows of Harvard College Cambridge, 1991).

Alexander Pope, An Essay on Man, I.292, (1733-34).

Alfred Marshall, Principles of Economics 685-86 (MacMilla, 8th ed. 1947).

Alvin E. Roth, Who Gets What-And Why?: The New Economics Of Matchmaking And Market Design, (Houghton Mifflin: New York 2015).

Apple, (2015), https://www.apple.com/supplier-responsibility/pdf/Apple_ Supplier_List_2015.pdf.

Apple's $10.5B on Robots to Lasers Shores Up Supply Chain, Bloomberg, (November 13, 2013), http://www.bloomberg.com/news/ articles/2013-11-13/apple-s-10-5b-on-robots-to-lasers-shores-up-supply-chain?cmpid=yhoo.

Automotive News Europe, http://europe.autonews.com/assets/PDF/CA62017619.PDF.

Brad Karp, Chair of Paul Weiss, Keynote Address at the Bloomberg Business of Law Summit (New York: June 2016).

Bruce MacEwen, A New Taxonomy: The Seven Law Firm Business Models, (New York, Adam Smith, Esq., LLC 2014).

Bruce MacEwen, Growth Is Dead: Now What? (New York, Adam Smith, Esq., LLC 2013).

Business Process Reengineering Assessment Guide, United States GAO, (May 1997), http://www.gao.gov/assets/80/76302.pdf.

Can Bots Fight Bullying, The New York Times, (September 21, 2016) http://www.nytimes.com/interactive/2016/09/20/insider/approve-or-reject-moderation-quiz.html.

Christopher Moyer, *How Google's Alpha Go Beat a World Go Champion*, (The Atlantic, March 28, 2016), http://www.theatlantic.com/technology/archive/2016/03/the-invisible-opponent/475611/.

Clayton M. Christensen, The Innovator's Dilemma: When New Technologies cause Great Firms to Fail, (Cambridge: Harvard Bus. Press 1997, 2d Ed. New York: 2011).

Council on Tall Buildings and Urban Habitat, *The Skyscraper Center*, (2016), https://www.skyscrapercenter.com/building/one-vanderbilt-place/15833.

David Wilkins and Maria Jose Esteban, *The Role of the Big Four Accountancy Firms in the Reconfiguration of the Global Market for Legal Services* (Harvard L. Sch. Ctr. on the Legal Prof., Working Paper 2016-01).

Dr. Larry Richard, *The Lawyer Personality: Why Lawyers are Skeptical*, ABA Legal Career Central, Nov. 16, 2015, http://www.abalcc.org/2015/11/16. the-lawyer-personality-why-lawyers-are-skeptical/.

Email from Dr. Larry Richard, to author (May 2016) (on file with author).

ESPN, (Dec. 11, 2015), http://espn.go.com/mlb/story/_/id/14330504/alex-rodriguez-252-million-contract-texas-rangers-remains-landmark-15th anniversary.

Erwin Smigel, The Wall Street Lawyer: Professional Organization Man? 34 n. 9, (Free Press of Glencoe/Collier Macmillan Limited 1964).

Exodus 32.

Farhad Manjoo, State of the Art: A High-Stakes Bet: Turning Google Assistant into a 'Star Trek' Computer, The New York Times, September 29, 2016 (emphasis mine), http://www.nytimes.com/2016/09/29/technology/google-assistant.html?ref=business&_r=0.

Fortune 500 (2006), http://archive.fortune.com/magazines/fortune/fortune500/full_list/ and 2016 at http://beta.fortune.com/fortune500/.

Frank H. Knight, Risk, Uncertainty and Profit 19 (Houghton Mifflin Co. 1921).

Geoffrey Moore, Crossing The Chasm: Marketing and Selling Disruptive Products to Mainstream Customers, (HarperCollins: New York, 1st ed. 1991, 3rd ed. 201).

George B. Shaw, Heartbreak House (1919).

George B. Shaw, Mrs. Warren's Profession (1893).

Google Brain Team, http://research.google.com/teams/brain/.

How & Where iPhone Is Made, CompareCamp, (September 17, 2014), http://comparecamp.com/how-where-iphone-is-made-comparison-of-apples-manufacturing-process/.

Higher Education in the Global Age: Policy, Practice and Promise in Emerging Societies 283 (Daniel Arya & Peter Marber eds. 2014).

How big would an iPhone 6 be if implemented using ENIAC technology, Reddit, (June 29, 2015), https://www.reddit.com/r/estimation/comments/3benfs/how_big_would_an_iphone_6_be_if_implemented_using/.

Insider: Approve or Reject These 5 Comments, The New York Times, (September 20, 2016), http://www.nytimes.com/interactive/2016/09/20/insider/approve-or-reject-moderation-quiz.html.

Interbrand, (2016), http://interbrand.com/best-brands/best-global-brands/2016/ranking/; and SAMSUNG (2016), http://www.samsung.co.kr/img/samsung/brand_4.pdf.

James Ashton, *Chris Saul Interview: Slaughter and May purrs like a Porsche but that doesn't mean we're run by Buff and Bertie*, The Independent, Nov. 23, 2014, http://www.independent.co.uk/news/people/profiles/chris-saul-interview-slaughter-and-may-purrs-like-a-porsche-but-that-doesn-t-mean-we-re-run-by-buffy-9878727.html.

Jewel Ward, *The Project Management Tree Swing Cartoon, Past and Present*, <tamingdata /> (August 7, 2010), http://www.tamingdata.com/2010/07/08/the-project-management-tree-swing-cartoon-past-and-present/).

John M. Keynes, *The Consequence to the Banks of the Collapse of Money Values*, in Essays in Persuasion 150 (1931).

John M. Keynes, The General Theory of Employment, Interest, and Money 113-14 (Palgrave Macmillan 1936).

John Naughton, *Thomas Kuhn: the man who changed the way the world looked at science*, The Guardian, (August 19, 2012): https://www. theguardian.com/science/2012/aug/19/thomas-kuhn-structure-scientific-revolutions.

Joseph Schumpeter, Capitalism, Socialism and Democracy 82 (Harper & Rowe: New York, 1942: 3d edition 1950).

Justin Fox, *Why Nokia Couldn't Beat the iPhone*, Bloomberg View, (October 18, 2016), https://www.bloomberg.com/view/articles/2016-10-18/why-nokia-couldn-t-beat-the-iphone (bold emphasis supplied).

Kindle, (Dec. 24, 2015, 7:07 AM), https://kdp.amazon.com/community/message.jspa?messageID=969951.

Kingsley Martin, *Artificial Intelligence: How will it affect legal practice – and when?*, Thomson Reuters Forum, (Vol. 2: Edition 1, 2016).

Letter from Voltaire, to Frederick William, Prince of Prussia (Nov. 28, 1770) (in Voltaire and his Letters 28 (S.G. Tallentyre ed. New York: G.P. Putnam's Sons 1919)).

Leslie Mitchell, Preface To Edmund Burke, Reflections on the Revolution in France, at i, (1790) (Oxford World Classics edition: Oxford University Press 2009).

Madeleine Falman, *Allen & Overy's Scott Zemser talks leveraged finance, lockstep and competing in the US*, Legal Bus. Blog, (August 26, 2016, 8:22PM) (emphasis supplied), http://www.legalbusiness.co.uk/index.php/lb-blog-view/7293-q-a-a-o-s-scott-zemser-talks-leveraged-finance-lockstep-and-competing-in-the-us.

Magic, Maths, And Money: The Relationship Between Science And Finance, what doux-commerce means to me, (August 2, 2013), http:magic-maths-money.blogspot.com/2013/08/what-doux-commerce-means-to-me.html.

Malcom Gladwell, *The Order of Things: What college rankings really tell us*, The New Yorker, (February 14 & 21, 2011), http://www.newyorker.com/magazine/2011/02/14/the-order-of-things.

Mark McAteer, *Global 100: Hitting the wall*, Legal Business (UK), (July 2016), http://www.legalbusiness.co.uk/index.php/analysis/6919-hitting-the-wall.

Mckinsey&Company, http://www.mckinsey.com/careers/explore-mckinsey.

Michael Hammer & James Champy, Reengineering The Corporation: A Manifesto For Business Revolution, (Harper Collins: New York, 1st ed. 1993, 2d ed. 2003).

Meinhard v. Salmon, 249 N.Y. 458, 164 N.E 545 (1928).

Mervyn King, The End Of Alchemy 133-34 (W.W. Norton & Co., Inc. 2016).

Michael Chui, et. al., Where machines could replace humans-- and where they can't (yet), McKinsey Quarterly, (July 2016), http://www.mckinsey.com/business-functions/digital-mckinsey/our-insights/where-machines-could-replace-humans-and-where-they-cant-yet.

N.C. St. Board of Dental Examiners v. Fed. Trade Comm'n, No. 13-534 (U.S. February 25, 2015), https://www.supremecourt.gov/opinions/14pdf/13-534_19m2.pdf.

Nassim N. Taleb, Antifragile: Things That Gain From Disorder, (Random House: New York) 2012.

Number of employees of the Big Four accounting/audit firms worldwide in 2015, Statista, https://www.statista.com/statistics/250503/big-four-accounting-firms-number-of-employees/.

Peter Lattman, *Dewey's Jeffrey Kessler Heading to Winston and Strawn,* Dealbook, (May 9, 2012), http://dealbook.nytimes.com/2012/05/09/deweys-jeffrey-kessler-heading-to-winston-strawn/.

Planning & Markets, *III. Moral Choice in the Private Property Order* (University of Southern California: Los Angeles, 1999), at http://www-pam.usc.edu/volume6/v6i1a2s3.htm.

Population for the 100 Largest Cities and Other Urban Places in the United States: 1790 to 1990, U.S. Census Bureau, https://www.census.gov/population/www/documentation/twps0027/twps0027.html.

Proskaur, http://www.proskauer.com/practices.

Radiant Law, "About Us," (October 2016), http://www.radiantlaw.com/about-us/.

Research at Google (undated), http://research.google.com/teams/brain/computer-systems/.

R. H. Frank, The Darwin Economy: Liberty, Competition, And The Common Good, (Princeton, Princeton University Press: 2011).

Richard Susskind, The Future Of The Professions: How Technology Will Transform The Work Of Experts (with Daniel Susskind, Oxford University Press: 2015).

Richard Susskind, Tomorrow's Lawyers: An Introduction To Your Future (Oxford University Press: 2013).

Richard Susskind, The End Of Lawyers? Rethinking The Nature Of Legal Services (Oxford University Press: 2008).

Richard Susskind, Transforming The Law: Essays On Technology, Justice And The Legal Marketplace (Oxford University Press: 2000).

Richard Susskind, The Future Of Law: Facing The Challenges Of Information Technology (Oxford University Press: 1996).

Richard Susskind, Essays On Law And Artificial '
1993).

Richard Susskind, Expert Systems In Law
1987).

Robert Frank & Philip Cook, The Winner-Take
Few at the Top get so much more than the rest
Penguin: 1996).

Robert Teitelbaum, Bloodsport: When Ruthless Dealmakers, Shı
Ideologies, And Brawling Lawyers Toppled The Corporate
Establishment 52 (New York: Public Affairs 2016) at 52, citing
Cary Reich, Financier: The Biography of Andre Meyer (New
York: John Wiley & Sons 1983).

Roger Lowenstein, *The Choice: To Squawk or to Go*, The Wall Street
Journal, (March 22, 2013), http://www.wsj.com/articles/SB10001
424127887323869604578370743034963414.

Ronald Coase: 1910 – 2013, Adam Smith, Esq., (September 3,
2013), http://adamsmithesq.com/2013/09/ronald-coase-1910-
2013/?single.

Ronald Coase, The Nature of the Firm, 4 Economica 386-405,
(1937), http://www3.nccu.edu.tw/~jsfeng/CPEC11.pdf.

Ronald J. Gilson, *The Legal Infrastructure of High Technology
Industrial Districts: Silicon Valley, Route 128, and Covenants Not
to Compete*, 74(3) N. Y. Univ. L. Rev. 575–629 (1999).

Rose Walker, *Ashurst partners agree to extend lockstep and introduce
bonus pool for star per-formers*, LegalWeek (August 2016),
http://www.legalweek.com/sites/legalweek/2016/08/02/ashurst-
extends-lockstep-and-introduces-bonus-pool/.

Sergio Marchionne says carmakers risk losing proprietary control,
Financial Times, (January 11, 2016), https://www.ft.com/
content/df1d7bb8-b889-11e5-bf7e-8a339b6f2164.

Rosen, *The Economics of Superstars*, 71 American Econ. Rev. -858 (1981), http://home.uchicago.edu/~vlima/courses/econ201/ uperstars.pdf.

encer Klaw, *The Wall Street Lawyers*, 57 Fortune 194, (1958).

Stephen F. Clark, 787 *Propulsion System*, Aeromagazine (3rd quarter 2012: Boeing corporation), http://www.boeing.com/commercial/ aeromagazine/articles/2012_q3/2/ (stating that Pratt & Whitney doe not supply engines for the 787).

Steven Kaplan & Joshua Rauh, *It's the Market: The Broad-Based Rise in the Return to Top Talent*, 27(3) J. Of Econ. Perspectives, 35-56 at 39 (2013).

Steve Kovalan, *Lateral Warfare*, ALM Legal Intelligence (July 2016), http:/ www.law.com/law/sites/ali/2016/07/21/lateral-warfare/.

Sue Michmerhuizen, *Confidentiality, Privilege: A Basic Value in Two Different Applications*, American Bar Association, (May 2007), http:// www.americanbar.org/content/dam/aba/administrative/professional responsibility/confidentiality_or_attorney.authcheckdam.pdf).

Susan T. Fiske & Cydney Dupree, *Gaining Trust as well as Respect in Communicating to Motivate Audiences about Science Topics*, PNAS 2014 111, April 2014, http://www.pnas.org/content/111/ Supplement_4/13593.abstract.

The American Lawyer's "AmLaw 200" for 2005 and 2015.

The Novus Approach, undated, http://novuslaw.com/approach/.

The Size of Boeing's Supply Chain, Actio, (January 19, 2015), http://blog. actio.net/supply-chain-management/the-size-of-boeing-supply/.

Thomas Kuhn, Structure of Scientific Revolutions, (University of Chicago Press, 1962, 4th ed. 2012).

The U.S. Bureau Of Economic Analysis, http://www.bea.gov/national/index.htm

Vault Top 100 2007, http://www.vault.com/company-rankings/law/vault-law-100/?sRankID=2&rYear=2007&pg=2 and at http://www.vault.com/company-rankings/law/vault-law-100/?pg=2.

Us Bureau Of Labor Statistics Data, GDPbyInd_VA_1947-2015.xlsx.

US quantitative measures worked in defiance of theory, Financial Times (October 13, 2014), https://www.ft.com/content/3b164d2e-4f03-11e4-9c88-00144feab7de.

Wendy Chang, *Time to regulate AI in the legal profession?*, Bloomberg Business of Law, (July 2016), https://bol.bna.com/time-to-regulate-ai-in-the-legal-profession-perspective/.

Wikipedia, Arnold Toynbee, https://en.wikipedia.org/wiki/Arnold_J._Toynbee.

Wikipedia, Colossus Computer, (undated), at: https://en.wikipedia.org/wiki/Colossus_computer.

Wikipedia, *Deep Blue versus Garry Kasparov*, https://en.wikipedia.org/wiki/Deep_Blue_versus_Garry_Kasparov.

William Henderson & Evan Parker, *The Diamond Law Firm: A New Model or the Pyramid Unraveling?*, Lawyer Metrics (Dec. 3, 2015), http://www.lawyermetrics.org/2013/12/03/the-diamond-law-firm-a-new-model-or-the-pyramid-unraveling/.

William Henderson, Variation in US News Reputation Over Time, Conglomerate Blog, (April 4, 2006), http://www.theconglomerate.org/2006/04/variation_in_us.html.

WSGR, https://wsgr.com/WSGR/DBIndex.aspx?SectionName=attorneys/results.htm (noting at pre-publication, the firm's website listed four partners under real estate, one of them retired).

About the Author

Bruce MacEwen

A lawyer and consultant to law firms on strategic and economic issues, since 2002 Bruce has been President of Adam Smith, Esq., an industry-leading management consultancy serving law firms around the globe.

The firm's site (adamsmithesq.com) features an online publication with a worldwide readership, comprising 15 years of archived articles on strategy, leadership, globalization, M&A, finance, compensation, cultural considerations, and partnership structures—totaling nearly 10,000 pages in print form.

In early 2013 Bruce published the book *"Growth Is Dead: Now What?,"* outlining the consequences for the legal industry of the great financial res of 2008, which Bloomberg Law immediately called "must-reading, from the one and only Bruce MacEwen."

Growth Is Dead was followed in 2014 by *"A New Taxonomy: The seven law firm business models,"* distinguishing among several fundamentally distinctive law firm types and describing the challenges and opportunities particular to each.

ruce has written for or been quoted in: *The New York Times; The Wall treet Journal; Fortune, Bloomberg; The American Lawyer*, and other ublications too numerous to mention. He is a sought-after speaker and equently appears at law firm retreats and legal industry conferences round the world.

reviously, Bruce:

- Practiced litigation and corporate law with Shea & Gould and with Breed, Abbott & Morgan in New York; and

- Practiced securities law in-house for nearly ten years at Morgan Stanley/Dean Witter on Wall Street.

- Bruce was educated at Princeton University (BA *magna cum laude* in economics) and at Stanford Law School (JD). He also completed the MBA coursework at NYU's Stern School of Business (evening program) while at Morgan Stanley.

native Manhattanite, he lives on New York's Upper West Side with is wife and their dog. He chairs the Finance Committee and serves as hancellor on the Vestry of St. Michael's Episcopal Church.

Notes

Made in the USA
Middletown, DE
17 March 2017